KV-637-980

STUDIES IN THE BRITISH ECONOMY SERIES

The United Kingdom Economy

The National Institute of Economic and Social Research
London

Contributors:

R. I. G. Allen
R. A. Batchelor
F. T. Blackaby
A. J. Brown
L. F. Campbell-Boross
A. J. H. Dean
K. Jones
R. L. Major
P. C. Meadows
A. D. Morgan
P. Mottershead
S. A. B. Page
R. W. R. Price
M. A. Utton
G. D. N. Worswick

Published on behalf of the Commission of the
European Communities by
HEINEMANN EDUCATIONAL
BOOKS LTD : LONDON

187834

Heinemann Educational Books Ltd
LONDON EDINBURGH MELBOURNE AUCKLAND TORONTO HONG KONG
SINGAPORE KUALA LUMPUR IBADAN NAIROBI JOHANNESBURG LUSAKA
NEW DELHI KINGSTON

ISBN 0 435 84575 6

ⓒ First edition the Commission of the European Communities
1975
ⓒ Additional material National Institute of Economic and
Social Research 1976, 1977
First published 1975
Second edition 1976
Third edition 1977

Published by Heinemann Educational Books Ltd
48 Charles Street, London W1X 8AH
Printed in Great Britain by
Biddles Ltd, Guildford, Surrey

CONTENTS

Prefaces vii

Chapter One GENERAL FEATURES
1. Introduction 1
2. Demographic trends 6
   The population 6
   Employment 10
3. National product and its uses 13
   United Kingdom output 13
   Output broken down by final demand 15
4. Regional differences 17

Chapter Two THE MAIN SECTORS
1. The industrial sector 29
   Industrial production 29
   Concentration 34
2. The services sector 41
3. The agricultural sector 45

Chapter Three SOCIAL ISSUES
1. Trade unions and labour relations 50
   Structure and organization 50
   Trade union objectives 51
   Trade unions and the government 52
   Trade unions and the law 53
2. Social policy 55
   Health and welfare services 55
   Education 57
   Income support 58
   Housing 59

Chapter Four
PUBLIC FINANCE AND NATIONALIZED INDUSTRIES
1. Changing patterns of public expenditure 61
2. Taxation 66
   Corporate taxation 68
   Selective employment tax 69
   Value-added tax 70
   Personal income and capital taxation 70
   North Sea oil and gas taxation 71
3. Nationalized industries 72

Chapter Five
FINANCIAL INSTITUTIONS AND MONETARY POLICY
1. Financial institutions   75
    The Bank of England   75
    The deposit institutions   76
    Other financial institutions   78
    Sources of funds for investment   79
2. Monetary policy   80
    Debt management   82
    The Treasury bill market   82
    The minimum lending rate   83
    Regulation of financial institutions   83
    Hire purchase controls   85

Chapter Six   EXTERNAL TRADE AND PAYMENTS
1. General structure of the balance of payments   86
2. The Commonwealth Preference and Sterling Area
    systems   88
3. Trade liberalization   91
4. Exchange rate policy   93
5. Imports and exports   95
6. Invisibles   102
7. Capital balance   103

Chapter Seven
THE MANAGEMENT OF THE BRITISH ECONOMY
1. Objectives   107
2. Institutions and instruments   109
3. The use of policy instruments   115
4. Attempts to break the pattern   116

Bibliography   121

Index   132

PREFACE TO THE FIRST EDITION

Following the establishment of the European Economic Community, a Committee of Experts was set up under the Chairmanship of Pierre Uri to prepare studies of the economic conditions of the member countries. The report on the economic situation in the countries of the Community was published in 1958. Following the accession in 1973 of Denmark, Ireland and the United Kingdom, the Commission of the European Communities considered that it would be valuable to supplement the Uri Report with a study on each of the new member States. On this occasion, however, the Commission followed a somewhat different procedure and commissioned separate studies from independent institutes in each of the three countries.

The present study of the United Kingdom was prepared at the National Institute of Economic and Social Research, London. The authors of the various chapters are named on the title page, but, in addition, mention should be made of the contributions of Miss G. I. Little, who prepared the text for publication and compiled the bibliography, and Miss S. Colwell, who typed the draft chapters as well as the final text. Thanks are due to Miss Patricia Brown of HM Treasury and her colleagues in government, as well as to H. R. Wortmann of the Commission of the European Communities, for valuable comments, and criticisms, of draft chapters. The responsibility for the final version remains with the authors.

G. D. N. Worswick
National Institute of Economic and Social Research
January 1975

PREFACE TO THIS EDITION

In this new edition the story and the figures have been brought up to date, which in most cases means the end of 1976. In a few instances up-dating required some rewriting of the text.

We are grateful to the Commission of the European Communities for allowing us to make the study available in the present form.

G. D. N. Worswick
National Institute of Economic and Social Research
May 1977

LIST OF TABLES

1.1 Populations of the United Kingdom and the United States compared, 1801-1976 *(p.1)*
1.2 The United Kingdom population, 1901-2011 *(p.7)*
1.3 The age composition of the United Kingdom population, 1911-2001 *(p.9)*
1.4 Working population and activity rates in the United Kingdom, 1901-71 *(p.10)*
1.5 United Kingdom GDP by industry *(p.14)*
1.6 United Kingdom expenditure and output at 1970 market prices, 1952-75 *(p.16)*
1.7 Rates of employment growth by region, 1921-61 *(p.19)*
2.1 United Kingdom industrial production (output) *(p.30)*
2.2 United Kingdom industrial production (inputs) *(p.32)*
2.3 United Kingdom employment in service industries compared with total in goods industries, 1969 and 1975 *(p.42)*
2.4 Annual average changes in productivity, 1951-66 *(p.44)*
2.5 Distribution of agricultural output, 1964-5 and 1975-6 *(p.46)*
2.6 Food imports by area of origin, 1972-5 *(p.48)*
3.1 Public expenditure on social services and housing (at current prices), 1951-75 *(p.56)*
4.1 Public expenditure in the United Kingdom as a proportion of GDP at factor cost, 1955-75 *(p.62)*
4.2 Tax revenue in the United Kingdom and the EEC as a proportion of GNP (at market prices) *(p.67)*
5.1 Deposit and secondary bank shares in total banking sector deposits and advances, 1963-74 *(p.77)*
5.2 Sources of capital funds of industrial and commercial companies, 1970-4 *(p.80)*
6.1 United Kingdom balance of payments, 1920-76 *(p.86)*
6.2 Imports of goods, 1900-76 *(p.96)*
6.3 Changes in the composition of imports, 1935-76 *(p.98)*
6.4 Changes in the area and commodity structures of exports, 1900-76 *(p.100)*
6.5 Exports of goods, 1900-76 *(p.102)*
6.6 External assets and liabilities, 1962 and 1975 *(p.104)*

Chapter One

GENERAL FEATURES

1. Introduction

In the nineteenth century the British economy was expanding in production, trade and overseas investment both in absolute terms and in its relative importance in the world. During the twentieth century, notwithstanding the setbacks of two world wars and the great depression, the upward trend in production and trade has been maintained, but outward investment has been increasingly offset by inward flows. In relation to the rest of the world, however, the story of production and trade has been one of fairly steady relative decline. Partly this is a simple matter of demography, which can most vividly be seen by comparing the populations of the United Kingdom and the United States over the whole period as in Table 1.1. Population movements alone made relative economic decline inevitable; but, in addition, the growth-rate of output per head in Britain has tended frequently to be somewhat lower than the average for other industrial countries of Western Europe and for the United States. This poor *relative* performance has been very much emphasized in the past twenty years, during which statistics of national product on a reasonably comparable basis have become increasingly available.

Britain was a pioneer, and for a long time the leader, in the process of industrialization which began at the end of the

Table 1.1. *Populations of the United Kingdom and the United States compared, 1801-1976*

				Millions
	1801	*1851*	*1901*	*1976*
United Kingdom	11.9	22.3	38.2	55.9
United States	5.5	24.1	77.6	215.1

eighteenth century. Already by the middle of the nineteenth century its urban population was as large as that remaining in the countryside, and from then on food and raw material needs for a growing population in industry were increasingly supplied from overseas in exchange for manufactured goods. By the end of the nineteenth century British exports provided one-third of the world's trade in manufactures. Throughout the nineteenth century there was also a net export of capital: at times a trickle, at others a torrent. To begin with it went mostly to Europe and the United States, then to Canada and India, and at the end of the century to Australia and Latin America. In the earlier stages money was invested mainly in public works, utilities and, above all, railways; later it was extended to industry and manufacturing enterprises. Besides money there was an increasing outflow of iron and steel, engineers, contractors and technology. In the decades before the First World War British overseas investment was of the same order, in *absolute amount,* as American private investment abroad in the 1960s. But already, at the height of its economic dominance, comments were being made which have become a commonplace today, that British industry was technically backward and was being overtaken by other countries, notably the United States and Germany.

The two world wars and the great depression administered great shocks to the world economy and to the British economy in particular, so that twentieth-century economic development cannot be easily summarized in a few simple trends. In particular, while the period between the two wars was one of small growth and high unemployment, the period after the Second World War was one of full employment and gradually accelerating growth. A single instance must suffice to illustrate this uneven development. In 1901 British steel output was just short of 5 million tons and in 1913 it had risen further to 7.7 million tons. Output fell immediately after the war, but this level was again surpassed in the late 1920s. However, in the early 1930s steel output was once again down to 5 million tons, no higher than it had been thirty years before. By contrast, after the Second World War the expansion of steel production, as indeed of many other industries, was strong; with output at 13 million tons just before the Second World War, it was over 20 million tons by the end of the 1950s.

Exports of manufactures reached a peak volume in 1913. The war sharply curtailed them and, even in the boom year of 1929, they had still not recovered their prewar level. The great depression dealt a further blow, as it did to world trade in general, so that British export levels in the early 1930s were little more than half those of 1913. But after the Second World War the recovery of exports was strong and continued; 1913 levels were surpassed in the early 1950s and since then there has been continuous growth. This uneven development in the twentieth century was, of course, matched in many other industrial countries. The *share* in world trade of British exports of manufactures started to fall at the beginning of this century; it jumped up again temporarily immediately after the Second World War while Germany and Japan were largely out of the picture. Thus, in 1950 the British share in exports of the main industrial countries was still 25.5 per cent, little short of the 27.3 per cent taken by the United States. But as Germany and Japan began their spectacular recoveries, the United Kingdom share started to fall once more, so that by 1960 it was down to 16 per cent and in 1973 for the first time it fell below 10 per cent.

The massive overseas investment at the beginning of this century dried up between the two wars, although it was to revive again after the Second World War until the most recent period. Meanwhile, dividends and interest from past investments played a significant role in the 1920s and 1930s in paying for necessary imports at a time when exports were performing none too well. During the Second World War large amounts of the investments were disposed of to pay for arms and when the war was over it was apparent that from then on current earnings from British exports, visible and invisible, would need to be at least sufficient to pay for current imports. The balance of payments has been a matter of concern for the economy in the past thirty years much more than in the previous century.

Judged by its own historical standards the economic performance of the United Kingdom in the past quarter of a century has been good. Unemployment was kept very low and the productivity of those employed rose annually at around 2 per cent in the early 1950s and at around 3 per cent in the early 1970s. This performance, however, appears in a different light when set against that of other industrial countries, most of which have had higher growth-rates, and some very much higher. Since 1973 growth has been interrupted and unemployment has risen substantially in the United Kingdom, as elsewhere.

The dominant economic philosophies in nineteenth-century Britain were *laissez-faire* and free trade. The major exception was in the monetary field, in which the Bank of England, though nominally remaining a private institution, emerged in a strong position of central control. Although mergers and industrial concentration were causing some concern at the end of the nineteenth century, there was no legislation laying down rules of competition of any general application until the 1950s. In the 1930s, however, there were several instances of specific government intervention to alleviate the problems of particular industries, especially the staple industries of the previous great industrial expansion, such as coal, cotton and shipbuilding, which were in decline. This growth of government intervention was closely associated with the abandonment of free trade in the 1930s. Since the Second World War there has been a considerable further increase in the role of the State in industry; important sectors such as transport, public utilities, coal and steel have been nationalized, and various forms of intervention and assistance for the private sector have been developed, especially in the context of regional policy; at the same time there has emerged a more systematic policy towards monopolies and restrictive trading agreements.

From the end of the Napoleonic Wars until the outbreak of the First World War the pound sterling was convertible into gold at a fixed rate which remained unchanged. After wartime suspension, convertibility was restored at the old rate in 1925, but this restoration was short-lived, the final break between sterling and gold being made in 1931. The gold standard, combined with complete freedom of movement of goods, services and people into and out of the country, had encouraged the growth in London of specialist banking, insurance and shipping firms able to arrange for the financing and movement of goods in almost any part of the world. In addition there developed important markets in many commodities. The business of the City of London has been, and still remains, an important influence towards internationalism in British economic policy.

The interests of industry and agriculture have not always pointed in the same direction. To begin with the advantage of cheap food, especially from the newly developing agricultural regions of North and South America and Australasia, outweighed any arguments in favour of protection. But the two world wars put a premium on protection of agriculture and the experience of mass unemployment in the 1920s, and especially the 1930s, reinforced other arguments in favour of protection for industry, which was finally introduced soon after the abandonment of the gold standard.

One consequence of the British decision to leave the gold

standard was to require those countries which had previously held their reserves in sterling (and thus indirectly in gold) to decide whether they wished to continue to hold reserves in sterling or to remain on the gold standard at the old rate. In the case of British colonies it was possible for this decision to be taken in London. The independent dominions, with the exception of Canada, decided to stay with sterling and so, for example, did the Scandinavian countries. This sterling block was the forerunner of the Sterling Area, which was formalized under the exchange control systems introduced during the Second World War. Partially overlapping with this Sterling Area was the Imperial Preference Area (subsequently the Commonwealth Preference Area), created at negotiations in Ottawa in 1932, the effect of which was to increase the share of both British exports to and British imports from Commonwealth countries.

Several, not always consistent, lines of thought lie behind British international economic policy in the past thirty years. The first was a desire to restore the importance of Britain in world trade and the world's monetary system. This led to support of the Bretton Woods monetary agreement and of the parallel Havana Charter of International Trade, which ultimately emerged in the more modest General Agreement on Tariffs and Trade (GATT). A premature attempt was made to restore full convertibility of sterling in 1947, but failed within a matter of weeks. Thereafter even the most ardent British advocates of the principles of Bretton Woods and GATT accepted that it might take some years before the various wartime controls of imports and monetary transactions could safely be removed altogether. It was not in fact until 1958 that one can say Britain was observing the full principles of the International Monetary Fund (IMF) and GATT.

A second strand of opinion was towards the maintenance, and if possible the strengthening, of the Commonwealth connection. Although many colonies were achieving political independence, it was thought that their economic development would be assisted by maintaining a close association with one another and with the United Kingdom. This Commonwealth approach was in some degree in conflict with the GATT philosophy which, while tolerant of customs unions, was hostile to preference areas.

The third line of thinking was the desire to secure closer economic relations with Europe, especially Western Europe. The idea of a free trade area for manufactures caught on quite early, particularly as it was felt to be consistent with other objectives,

5

such as those of GATT. There was less universal support for other aspects of the original EEC such as the Common Agricultural Policy, partly because it was thought that it would favour the abandonment of a historic policy of cheap food, also that it was in conflict with the Commonwealth commitment.

There are still conflicting tendencies in the formation of British international economic policy at the present time and the rise in the price of oil since 1973 has added a new dimension, as it has for the rest of the world. There seems now to be fairly general agreement that the attempt to maintain a major key currency role for sterling was a burden on the British economy too great for it to stand and that future British external policies should have more modest aims.

British domestic policy since the war has been to secure the establishment of a welfare state. The first requirement of this was the maintenance of full employment, an objective which seemed never to be seriously threatened until the 1970s, but which has been put in question by the energy crisis and the sharp increase in the rate of inflation which has occurred throughout the industrial world. There has been a great extension of social services, in health and education especially, while industrial policy has been based upon the concept of a 'mixed economy' of private and public enterprises. For a long time after the war the two major political parties, both of which formed several governments, appeared in practice tacitly to accept a common central programme with differences of emphasis. In the past five years, however, the power in the two main parties may have been shifting away from the centre in opposite directions. The years ahead will show whether some radical transformation in British industry and society is about to occur or whether some new consensus will emerge.

2. Demographic Trends

The population

In comparison with the very rapid expansion of population which took place in the nineteenth century, there has been a relatively slow increase throughout this century. From 1801 until 1911 the population increased in each decade by at least 10 per cent, but since 1911 the increase in each decade has never been more than about 5 per cent. The natural increase in population was at its highest in absolute terms from 1901 to 1911, when births exceeded deaths by 4.7 million. In the interwar years the net increase fell to 2.0 million (1921-31) and then 1.8 million (1931-41). Since the war

Table 1.2. *The United Kingdom population, 1901-2011*

	Home population (000s)	Increase Absolute (000s)	Increase Percentage (%)	Net immigration[a] (000s)
1901	38,237	3,845	10.1	−820
1911	42,082	1,945	4.6	−919
1921	44,027	2,011	4.6	−672
1931	46,038			
1941	n.a.	4,187	9.1	+435
1951	50,225	2,484	4.9	+ 57
1961	52,709	2,806	5.3	−428
1971	55,515	220[c]	0.4	−560
1981	55,911[b]	1,377	2.5	−320
1991	57,288[b]	1,057	1.8	−320
2001	58,345[b]	680	1.2	−320
2011	59,025[b]			

SOURCE: CSO, *Annual Abstract of Statistics, 1976.*

[a]Including various adjustments for the visitor balance and armed forces living abroad.

[b]Projections of mid-year 'total population'.

[c]Not equal to the difference between the figures in the first column because of changes in definition.

the net decadal increases have been 2.5 million (1951-61) and 2.8 million (1961-71). The increase in population over those last ten years was 5.3 per cent, which is slightly higher than the increase of 4.9 per cent in the 1950s (see Table 1.2), but official projections of the population over the next four decades from 1971 expect a slower rate of increase of 0.4 per cent (1971-81), 2.5 per cent (1981-91), 1.8 per cent (1991-2001) and 1.2 per cent (2001-11).[1] These projections mean that the population of the United Kingdom, estimated to be 56.0 million in mid-1975, would fall to 55.9 million by 1981, but rise to 59.0 million by 2011. However, such projections are constantly changed. The birthrate in recent years has been

1Central Statistical Office, *Annual Abstract of Statistics, 1976,* London, HMSO, 1976, table 6.

falling much more sharply than expected by those who prepared the official projections, so that with each successive fall the projections of future population have been brought down. The laws concerning abortion have recently been changed, and the principle of the free provision of contraceptives has been spreading. It is therefore highly uncertain what the average completed family size will be for couples now in their twenties and thirties. In 1975 the official projection for the increase in population in the last quarter of the century was $3\frac{3}{4}$ million. In the following year it had already been revised downwards to less than $2\frac{1}{2}$ million and may be changed again.

Migration, both inward and outward, has been an important influence on United Kingdom population. For the first thirty years of this century there was an average net emigration of almost 100,000 a year; in the next ten years (1931-41) there was a net inflow of 600,000. During the 1950s there was an almost equal balance between emigration and immigration—a net inward balance of 57,000 over the ten years 1951-61. A large number of the immigrants came from the West Indies, East and West Africa, and India and Pakistan, but there were always large numbers of Irish immigrants as well. Since the Commonwealth Immigrants Act of 1962 and further restrictive measures which followed it, immigration has been severely restricted and outward migration has considerably exceeded immigration. Over the decade 1961-71 there was a net emigration of 428,000, but this figure masks the yearly movements; in 1961-2 there was a net inflow of 300,000, whilst since 1962 there has been a large net outflow of, on average, some 60,000 persons a year. The official population projections assume a future net outflow averaging about 56,000 a year in 1971-81 and a further 32,000 a year to the end of the century.

The female population continues to be larger than the male, despite the greater number of male births (outweighing female births in the ratio of 1.06 to 1), because of the higher male mortality, but the gap between males and females is narrowing. The 1951 population was 48.0 per cent male, so that there were 4 per cent more females than males; by 1971 this gap had narrowed to 2.8 per cent, with 48.6 per cent males; the projections for 2001 indicate a male population of 49.3 per cent and hence a gap of only 1.4 per cent. For all age groups under 45 the male population now outnumbers the female population, although in no case by more than about 6 per cent. In the older age groups the position is reversed and females outnumber males by successively greater amounts.

Table 1.3. *The age composition of the United Kingdom population, 1911-2001*

| | Absolute size | | | Proportion of total | | |
	Under 15	15-64 *(millions)*	65+	Under 15	15-64 *(percentages)*	65+
1911	13.0	26.9	2.2	30.9	63.9	5.2
1931	11.1	31.4	3.4	24.2	68.4	7.4
1951	11.3	33.4	5.5	22.5	66.5	11.0
1961	12.3	34.1	6.1	23.4	64.9	11.7
1971	13.6	35.4	7.3	24.2	62.9	12.9
1981[a]	*11.5*	*36.2*	*8.3*	*20.5*	*64.6*	*14.9*
1991[a]	*11.9*	*37.0*	*8.4*	*20.8*	*64.6*	*14.6*
2001[a]	*12.6*	*37.6*	*8.1*	*21.6*	*64.5*	*13.9*

SOURCE: CSO, *Annual Abstract of Statistics, 1976,* Table 15.
[a]Projections of total population at mid-year.

The age composition of the United Kingdom population has changed quite radically through this century. Partly because of successively longer life expectancies, the proportion of people aged 65 and over has been rising. In 1911 5.2 per cent of the population were aged 65 and over; by 1971 this figure was 12.9 per cent. It is expected to continue to rise but then fall back to around 14 per cent by the end of the century (see Table 1.3). The corollary to this is that the proportion of people under 65 years of age has fallen and, because the trend since the war has been for the proportion of the population aged under 15 to increase slowly (22.5 per cent in 1951, but 24.2 per cent in 1971), this has meant that the proportion of the population aged 15-64 has fallen substantially, from 66.5 per cent in 1951 to 62.9 per cent in 1971. In other words, since the war the population has tended to become both top- and bottom-heavy. This is regarded as unfavourable in so far as it means that the part of the population which is of working age has shrunk, but this unfavourable trend is not expected to persist. It had two causes: first, the low interwar birth rate, which has meant a relative decline in the number of middle-aged persons, and, secondly, the slightly higher birth rate of the late 1950s and the 1960s. The first will eventually result in a fall in the proportion of the old, whilst the second has been reversed in just the last few years. The second will also mean that more people will come of working age in the 1970s. These factors taken together mean that the forty-year decline in the proportion of 15-64 year olds in the population will be reversed in the mid-1970s. Official projections suggest that this proportion will rise from its 1971 level of 62.9 per cent (a historic low) to 64.6 per cent in 1981 and be at 64.5 per cent by 2001. One cannot put much confidence in these projections, but one can at least say that the unfavourable movement in the age structure should now come to an end.

Employment

The changing demographic structure of the population, as indicated, has meant that since the 1930s a decreasing proportion of the population has been of working age. This is one of the reasons why the working population has not kept pace with the growth in the total population. In recent years the working population has not only declined as a proportion of total population but has also declined in absolute terms (see Table 1.4). Several further reasons have been put forward to explain why this has happened. The main arguments concern, first, the marked trend in the number of young

Table 1.4. *Working population and activity rates in the United Kingdom, 1901-71*

	Working population (thousands)	Activity rates							
		Males and females					Females		
		15-19	20-24	25-44	45-64	65+ (percentages)	20-24	25-44	45-64
1901	18,280	n.a.ᵃ	76.0	61.1	55.5	34.1	56.7	27.2	21.1
1931	20,930	77.6	80.7	62.5	54.7	25.3	65.1	30.9	19.6
1951	23,809	81.3	79.7	66.7	59.5	15.9	65.4	36.1	28.7
1961	25,345	72.9	76.8	69.4	66.0	12.7	62.0	40.8	37.1
1966	26,174	68.6	77.2	72.6	60.6	13.1	61.6	47.1	46.1
1971	25,421	58.4	75.1	74.4	71.5	11.3	60.1	50.6	50.2

SOURCES: Department of Employment, *British Labour Statistics: historical abstract 1886-1968*, London, HMSO, 1971; *Department of Employment Gazette*, November 1973.

ᵃStatistics not available because of uncertainty over ages at which juveniles started work.

people who are continuing their education beyond the minimum school-leaving age and, secondly, variations in participation rates.

The proportion of the population in the age group 15-19 attending grant-aided schools in Great Britain has risen from 9 per cent in 1951 to just over 25 per cent in 1972. Furthermore, since 1972 the minimum school-leaving age has been raised from 15 to 16, which means that an estimated further 0.4 per cent of the total population has been removed from the working population. Besides this increase in the amount of schooling undertaken beyond the age of 14, there has been a rapid expansion of full-time further education. In particular, there has been a boom in university education, especially in the last ten years. The number of full-time students at United Kingdom universities rose from 87,000 in 1951-2 to 117,000 in 1961-2, and then more than doubled in the next ten years to 243,000 in 1971-2. A similar expansion took place in other establishments of further education. The result has been that a very considerable number of young persons who would previously have been entering the work-force are now continuing with their education. This trend is reflected in the activity rates for the 15-19 age group: in 1951 81.3 per cent of this group were economically active; this fell to 72.9 per cent in 1961 and to 58.4 per cent in 1971.

An examination of activity rates for different age groups (as in Table 1.4) shows that, although since the war the proportion of persons economically active has declined for those aged under 25 and for those over 64, nevertheless the 25-64 age group has increased its rate of activity quite substantially. In particular there has been a large and continuing increase in the proportion of women aged 25-64 in the work-force. This has mainly been due to the much higher number of married women who now work; since 1931 their activity rate has increased from 10 per cent to nearly 50 per cent. This increase in the female participation rate meant that the percentage of women in the total working population increased from 32.0 per cent in 1951 to 36.0 per cent in 1971. Yet, despite this large increase in female participation, the working population has still been a declining proportion of the total population, because the lower participation of the younger and older age groups has proved a stronger force. Indeed these latter effects have been so strong that the total working population has declined in absolute terms since 1966. However, as the age structure of the population 'improves' through the 1970s, this trend may well be reversed.

Unemployment, which was rarely less than 10 per cent throughout the interwar years, has normally been below 3 per cent

11

and rose above 4 per cent for the first time since the war only in mid-1975. Nevertheless, there has been a slow secular movement towards higher levels of unemployment throughout the postwar period; the peak level has slowly risen through successive cycles. In the early 1950s the peak rate was 2.2 per cent (1952); but in the 1967-73 cycle this had risen to 3.9 per cent (1972), and in the present cycle has risen above $5\frac{1}{2}$ per cent (1977). Similarly at troughs, the unemployment rate has tended to move upwards through successive cycles. Various reasons have been put forward to explain this phenomenon: it is thought that higher unemployment compensation and compulsory redundancy payments have meant that the unemployed worker is not faced with the same urgency to find a job as in the past; it is also thought that firms may now carry fewer under-employed staff, especially in slack periods. There has also been a noticeable rise in graduate unemployment, particularly amongst social scientists, but it is not certain how far this reflects an over-supply of new graduates, or how far it is the outcome of an unwillingness to take up employment immediately after graduation.

A feature of the unemployment pattern is the great disparity between the various regions. Northern Ireland, for instance, has consistently had a much higher rate of unemployment than the rest of the United Kingdom. In 1972, whilst the average rate of unemployment for the United Kingdom was 3.9 per cent, that for Northern Ireland was 8.0 per cent. Two other regions, Scotland and the North of England, have also tended to have rates of unemployment well above the average—in 1972 rates of 6.4 and 6.3 per cent respectively. This is in sharp contrast to the South East where, until 1975, unemployment has never been more than 2.1 per cent (1972) in the postwar period and has at times been less than 1.0 per cent, for example in 1964-6. East Anglia, the Midlands and the South West have also been areas where unemployment has been much less than the national average. These regional disparities have been partly the result of the decline of the older consumer goods industries, such as textiles and clothing, and of mining, shipbuilding and other heavy industries, all of which have been concentrated in the regions such as Scotland, the North, the North West and Wales which now exhibit above-average unemployment levels. In these less prosperous regions there is a lower activity rate and a much smaller proportion of female manual workers than in the rest of the country. Although there is only a rather slow movement of the population within the United Kingdom, it is noticeable that the movement is towards areas of high incomes and job vacancies (the South East and the Midlands) and away from areas of low incomes and higher unemployment (especially Northern Ireland, Scotland and Wales).

3. National Product and its Uses

United Kingdom output
Since the war the average growth-rate of GDP for the United Kingdom has been about 2½ per cent per annum. This is higher than at any other comparable period this century, but is nevertheless lower than that of all other major industrialized countries. There has been a marked cyclical pattern in the rate of growth, but only four years of actual decline (1952, 1958, 1974 and 1975). There have been six cycles over the last twenty years: 1951-5, 1955-60, 1960-5, 1965-9, 1969-73 and the present cycle from 1973.[1] Nevertheless the trend rate of growth has remained fairly constant.

Growth-rates in individual sectors have differed widely from the overall average (Table 1.5). There has been an absolute decline in the mining and quarrying sector, which was at a postwar peak in 1954 but has been running down ever since at a rate of over 2 per cent each year. This trend will be reversed in the later 1970s, however, since the output of North Sea oil from British fields will be recorded in the industrial production statistics in the mining and quarrying sector. There are also plans, in the light of the oil price rise and the energy situation generally, to increase coal output in the next few years from the present 120 million tons annually to 150 million tons.

Construction has been an industry which has grown very slowly since the war, and it has actually shown a marginal decline over the period 1965-75. Public administration and defence has also grown slowly, although the size of the public sector as a whole has grown substantially. Other sectors which have grown at less than the national average are the 'ownership of dwellings' and 'miscellaneous services'.

Output of the manufacturing sector has grown at a rate of 2.3 per cent per annum over the period 1955-75. Within the sector

[1] Peak to peak. The dating of these cycles is taken from D. J. O'Dea, *Cyclical Indicators for the Postwar British Economy,* Cambridge University Press, 1975.

Table 1.5. *United Kingdom GDP by industry*

| | GDP 1975 | | Annual growth-rates | |
	Value (£m)	Proportion of total (%)	1955-75 (%)	1965-75 (%)
Agriculture, forestry and fishing	2,527	2.6	2.4	1.8
Mining and quarrying	1,645	1.7	−2.4	−3.4
Manufacturing	26,726	27.9	2.3	1.5
Construction	6,411	6.7	1.8	−0.2
Gas, electricity and water	2,866	3.0	4.7	4.2
Transport	5,753	6.0 ⎫	2.6	2.9
Communication	2,809	2.9 ⎭		
Distributive trades	9,159	9.6	2.4	1.9
Insurance, banking and finance	7,727	8.1	4.8	5.1
Ownership of dwellings	5,535	5.8	2.1	2.4
Public administration and defence	7,107	7.4	—	0.6
Professional and scientific services ⎱	17,584	18.3	⎰ 3.4	3.4
Miscellaneous services ⎰			⎱ 1.6	0.7
Total	95,849	100.0		
Residual error	920			
Adjustment for financial services	−3,623			
GDP at factor cost	93,146		2.3	1.8

SOURCE: CSO, *National Income and Expenditure,* London HMSO, (annual).

particular industries have grown at very disparate rates and these are examined in the following section. The largest growth-rates, however, have been recorded in non-manufacturing; gas, electricity and water have grown by 4.7 per cent per annum, whilst insurance, banking and finance have grown by 4.8 per cent per annum. This latter sector has been growing particularly fast in recent years, and this partly reflects the continuing rapid expansion of world trade, in which the City plays an important servicing role. The sector now constitutes 8.1 per cent of total output (1975 figures) compared with 27.9 per cent for manufacturing and 39.3 per cent for total industrial production. Agriculture, forestry and fishing have now shrunk to providing only 2.6 per cent of output, and mining and quarrying to 1.7 per cent. Public administration, defence, health and education now provide 14 per cent and transport, communication and the distributive trades nearly 20 per cent of output—roughly the same share as in 1950. The ownership of dwellings, at 5.8 per cent, is now a more important component of output than it used to be, whilst construction, at 6.7 per cent, has about the same importance.

Productivity changes in these various sectors have meant that the pattern of employment has not necessarily mirrored the changes in output. Although agriculture has continued to grow, its total labour force (employers and employees) has more than halved from about 1.5 million in 1950 to only 700,000 in 1974. In the same period employment in all service industries (SIC Orders XXII-XXVII) has risen from 8.9 to 12.5 million. Whilst agriculture has undoubtedly seen a very rapid rise in productivity, in services productivity has increased only slowly. There has also been a decline between 1950 and 1974 in the numbers employed in manufacturing, and that sector now accounts for 34.5 per cent of the total numbers in civil employment, whereas previously it accounted for 41.0 per cent. Since output in manufacturing was growing faster than average over the period, this reflects a substantial increase in productivity in the sector. Another particularly productive sector has been gas, electricity and water, where the numbers employed have fallen only slightly and output has grown rapidly. In mining and quarrying there has been a large fall in employment, from 855,000 in 1950 to 335,000 in 1974; this reflects not only the large fall in output in this declining sector, but also a marked rise in productivity. Despite the large increase in government work, the number of employees in the public sector (public corporations, central and local government) has risen little, from 6.2 million in 1950 to 6.8 million in 1974, although in the earlier year there was still a large residue of the wartime civil service.

Output broken down by final demand

Slightly more than half of total final expenditure (50.7 per cent in 1975) is accounted for by consumption, but the proportion has been slowly declining since the 1950s (Table 1.6). Both investment and exports have been increasingly important components of final expenditure, with investment increasing its share from 9.7 per cent to 14.3 per cent and exports from 14.8 per cent to 20.5 per cent between 1952 and 1975. The other major component of demand, public authorities' current expenditure, has shown a large fall in its relative share, from 21.0 per cent in 1952 to 15.5 per cent in 1975; this is largely explained by the falling proportion of output taken

15

Table 1.6. *United Kingdom expenditure and output at 1970 market prices, 1952-75*

| | Contribution to final demand | | | | | Value |
| | 1952 | 1962 | 1967 | 1972 | 1975 | 1975 |
			(percentages)			*(£m)*
Consumers' expenditure	54.3	54.9	52.7	51.9	50.7	35,374
Public authorities current expenditure	21.0	16.5	16.0	14.7	15.5	10,807
Gross domestic fixed capital formation	9.7	13.3	15.2	14.8	14.3	9,967
Stockbuilding	0.2	—	0.6	—	−1.0	−699
Exports of goods and services	14.8	15.3	15.5	18.6	20.5	14,290
Total final expenditure	100.0	100.0	100.0	100.0	100.0	69,739
Less imports of goods and services						13,503
GDP at market prices						56,236

SOURCE: CSO, *National Income and Expenditure* (various issues).

by military defence. However, this masks the position of the public sector as a whole, which has grown in importance since the 1950s. When transfer payments like debt interest, pensions, social security payments and grants to industry are included, the public sector now controls, directly and indirectly, the way in which half of the national product is spent. The rise in public spending on this wider definition has been especially rapid during the 1960s; in 1964 public spending as a share of GDP (at current prices) was 43.6 per cent, by 1967 this had risen to 50.1 per cent and by 1975 it was 58.5 per cent. The change in the importance of the public sector is examined in greater detail in Chapter 4.

The trend in consumers' expenditure since the early 1960s has been for a relative decline in spending on the necessities — food, clothing, housing, fuel and light — and for greater spending on consumer durables. At 1970 prices, household expenditure on food declined quite sharply from 21.3 per cent of consumption in 1965 to 18.0 per cent in 1975; spending on drink and tobacco has marginally increased its relative share in consumption over the same period (rising from 12.3 per cent to 13.7 per cent), but this disguises the rapid growth in consumption of wines and spirits, and the actual decline in the sales of tobacco up until 1971. Similarly, the increase in expenditure on durables, from 7.5 to 8.4 per cent, masks a static share of furniture sales and a large rise in spending on cars, motor cycles and radio and electrical goods.

4. Regional Differences

The regions into which the United Kingdom is divided for statistical purposes are Northern Ireland, Scotland, Wales and eight standard regions of England. They are so delimited that most of them contain a major urban core (sometimes a double one) and in no region is the population predominantly rural. Although it is still possible (notably in the Highlands and Islands of Scotland) to find quite extensive rural areas where agriculture is the largest single occupation, the regions with the largest reliance upon agriculture are Northern Ireland and East Anglia, neither with more than 10 per cent of their active population in this pursuit. The dichotomy, so important in many countries, between predominantly agricultural and non-agricultural major regions does not exist in the United Kingdom.

The historical origin of the differences in structure and prosperity between the regions is to be found in developments during and since the Industrial Revolution. The urbanization which has been proceeding at varying rates for at least four centuries has brought a continuous increase in the proportion of the total population in and around London, which now dominates an extensive city region — the South East — containing almost a third of that total. From the mid-eighteenth century, however, until the beginning of the twentieth, a proportionately more rapid growth took place in industrial areas outside the South East, based in many instances upon coalfields. The most spectacular development was in the North West, based largely upon the cotton textile industry, followed by Yorkshire and Humberside (wool textiles, steel and coal) and the West Midlands (metal working). The North (coal, steel and shipbuilding) and Wales (coal and steel) followed long-term trends in growth not very different from that of the country as a whole. Scotland and Northern Ireland, despite very substantial industrialization, declined in population in relation to the United Kingdom total — Northern Ireland for a long time declined absolutely. Throughout this period up to the First World War, the industrial regions of Wales, the Midlands and the North of

England drew in a net immigration of population, or suffered less from emigration overseas than did the less industrialized regions of the South West and East Anglia; they also seem to have had higher wage levels and (in the early twentieth century) lower unemployment. Scotland and Northern Ireland, with, at that time, still large populations in low-income agriculture, continued long-established traditions of heavy outward migration, largely overseas.

The industrial areas outside the South East had owed their growth in the main to foreign trade and shipbuilding. However, the heavy British commitment to foreign trade, prolonged in the face of rising foreign competition by massive overseas lending, was sharply checked by the First World War and its aftermath. The effects of this check were especially concentrated on those regions in which the old exporting industries were localized. How far a region's departure from the national trends of growth in employment is attributable to its structure — its concentration on industries that nationally have fared markedly better or worse than all industries taken together — is a question to which there is no unambiguous answer when, as is normally the case, the entities described for statistical purposes as the same 'industry' in different regions both grow at different rates and, indeed, are generally very imperfectly comparable in what they actually produce. Nevertheless, on any reasonable interpretation, the relative depression of these industrialized areas in the last fifty years has been due primarily to their inherited industrial structure. It is not only their original reliance upon industries that have suffered in world markets that is concerned; the rapid growth in the last two generations has, to a large extent, been in non-manufacturing activities, of which a substantial part (central government, professional and scientific services, head office activities, the handling of air traffic, entertainment, specialized aspects of banking and finance) has a strong tendency to establish itself near the national capital. Another rapid grower, the motor vehicle industry, found in the West Midlands and the South East the varied metal-working activities best suited to providing its components, and thus increased still more the relative disadvantage of the regions further north. Moreover, once differences of prosperity are established various forces operate to accentuate them. Some of these are greatly reduced in the United Kingdom by the extent to which a progressive tax system and central provision of social services and infrastructure prevent poorer regions from falling behind in the facilities they offer, but old industrial regions with low growth-rates almost inevitably present a less attractive appearance to new industry than fast-growing ones, or those regions like the South West and East Anglia with in most parts little industrial dereliction.

Table 1.7. *Rates of employment growth by region, 1921-61*

	Percentages
North	10.8
Yorks. and Humberside	7.9
North West	1.3
East Midlands	26.5
West Midlands	39.9
East Anglia	20.4
South East	41.3
South West	29.3
Wales	0.3
Scotland	1.0
Northern Ireland	−4.6[a]

[a]For the period 1926-61.

The result of these circumstances is that the regions north of the Trent and west of the Severn have suffered a shortage of new jobs in relation to the increase in their indigenous population of working age; the rest, except in times of industrial recession, have experienced the opposite maladjustment. The less prosperous regions have accordingly shown slower growth of total employment, lower income levels, higher unemployment and net outward migration in comparison with the more prosperous. These differences may now be briefly described.

It will be seen from Table 1.7 that, over the period 1921-61 as a whole, only Northern Ireland suffered an actual decline in employment (although Wales suffered quite a severe one briefly between the two world wars), but that Wales, Scotland and the North West experienced virtually no growth, in sharp contrast to the 40 per cent growth of the South East and the West Midlands. More recently the relative records of the regions have been broadly

19

the same as before, except that the South West and East Anglia have moved up to become the fastest growers, largely taking overspill from the South East, and that Northern Ireland, up to 1969, had so far improved as to show a faster growth of employment than Great Britain, although the natural increase in its population had grown still more.

Differences of income *per capita* between regions are smaller in the United Kingdom than in most other countries; only Northern Ireland shows a really large departure from the national average. In factor income *per capita* Northern Ireland stands some 36 per cent below the average, but all the other regions lie within about 12 per cent above or below it. The differences (including the Northern Ireland deficiency) are in part due to differences in the proportion of population that is of working age and in part to differences in the rate of participation in the labour force by those of working age. In productivity per person in work Northern Ireland lies only 23 per cent below average and the other regions range from about 9 per cent below to 6 per cent above. But the interregional flow of property incomes, which is quite strongly in favour of the richest region (the South East) as well as of one of the otherwise poorer ones (the South West), makes the range of gross regional product *per capita* somewhat greater than that of domestic factor incomes.

The distribution of expenditure is, however, markedly affected by taxation and those parts of public spending that can be identified as being mainly beneficial to particular regions; also by private capital transfers. It is further modified in real terms by the fact that the general price level is appreciably higher in London and the South East than elsewhere, mostly because of the higher costs of accommodation and travel to work. When all this is taken into account, it seems that real expenditure per head is considerably less than 20 per cent below the national average in Northern Ireland and elsewhere ranges from perhaps 10 per cent below to 8 per cent above.

This relatively high degree of interregional uniformity of income and expenditure levels is attributable in the first place to the absence of a division of regions into urban and rural which has already been mentioned. Agriculture, as happens in other countries also, is outstandingly the least well paid occupation, but it does not bulk large enough in any United Kingdom region either to pull the average down very far arithmetically, or to depress earnings in other industries very much through market forces. Moreover, the compactness of the United Kingdom and the national scope of much collective bargaining in its labour market tend to standardize wages in an industry across the different regions. In general, the industrial mix rarely accounts for much of the excess or deficiency of a region's earnings level in comparison with the national average. The part played by the high degree of centralization of public finance has already been mentioned.

In unemployment levels the interregional differences are much more important; indeed, it may be argued that the tendency to interregional standardization of the price of labour makes deficiency of regional demand manifest itself in unemployment rather than in low wages. Between the two world wars, when unemployment was high nationally, it stood in the most depressed regions at something like twice the national average. A not dissimilar relationship (with proportionate differences in unemployment rates, indeed, rather greater) has persisted in the period of lower unemployment since the Second World War — rates of about 1 per cent in the South East and the West Midlands, 2 or 3 per cent in the North, 3 or 4 per cent in Scotland and 6 or 7 per cent in Northern Ireland are typical of considerable periods before 1966, since when the general rate has stood higher, but the relative (though not the absolute) interregional differences have been rather smaller. In general, regional unemployment rates vary inversely with growth-rates of employment, though with some anomalies; Yorkshire and Humberside, for instance, has generally shown slow growth and low unemployment, and the South West rapid growth and a rather higher unemployment rate.

The recorded rates of registered unemployment do not tell the whole story. According to Census data, there is a body of unregistered unemployed so distributed between regions as to raise considerably the absolute, but not the relative, interregional differences in the incidence of involuntary worklessness. More important quantitatively, however, is the wide interregional variation in participation rates of women in the labour force — varying from under 30 to nearly 45 per cent. To a large extent these variations are explained by the localization of traditionally female-employing and male-employing occupations, but to some degree the incidental effect of this localization is to reduce the participation rate in regions of low general demand: Wales, the North and Scotland in particular. It also seems to be true that high effective demand for labour, as in the South East and the West Midlands, has the effect one would expect in increasing the participation rate, although the trend over recent decades has generally been for that rate to increase fastest where it initially stood lowest. Diversification of the occupational structure must be responsible for much of this.

The question arises how far the higher unemployment in the north and in parts of the west of the United Kingdom does, in fact, as has been implied here, stem from shortage of effective demand in those regions, and how far it arises from greater imperfection of their labour markets. It seems that the regions where the rate of change of the industrial structure is greatest, and those where population and industry are most widely dispersed, have some tendency to higher levels of unemployment, presumably due to market imperfection. Seasonal unemployment is also higher in some places than others, although the differences are more apparent at sub-regional than at regional level. But the evidence suggests that considerably the greater part of interregional differences in the unemployment rate is to be attributed to variations in the level of effective demand, rather than to differences in labour-market imperfection or in the incidence of inherent unemployability in the labour force.

Some reference has already been made to aspects of the pattern of interregional migration. The largest population movements have been relatively short-distance ones out of the conurbations and large cities, but these have mostly intra-regional rather than interregional significance. Interregionally, the *net* internal movements, which consist of differences between gross inward and outward movements several times as large, have followed a fairly simple pattern. Every region has gained from those to the north of it and lost to those to the south, except for large net movements from the South East to the neighbouring regions, East Anglia, the East Midlands and the South West. The last mentioned region is the only one that has tended to show a net gain from every other one; Scotland is the only one except for Northern Ireland that has lost to every other. The effects of these internal movements have been reinforced in general by the fact that nearly every region of England and Wales has gained from overseas migration (with the South East and the West Midlands gaining most), while Scotland has lost heavily. Taking internal and overseas movements together, Scotland in the 1960s lost more than 6 per thousand of her population a year (almost equal to her natural increase), Northern Ireland lost more than 5 per thousand (50 per cent of natural increase) and the North 3 per thousand (60 per cent of natural increase). The South West and East Anglia were gaining from migration at about the same proportional rate as that at which Scotland was losing; the South East and the West Midlands had become slight net losers.

In general, gross interregional migration movements (leaving overseas movements out of account) seem to be reasonably well 'explained' statistically by the sizes of existing populations in the regions of origin and destination, the existence or non-existence of proximity between them, and their unemployment rates. The effect of the last mentioned variable is roughly that for every percentage point by which the unemployment in a region rises above the national average it may expect an additional net loss annually of something between 2 and 5 per thousand of its male population of working age. The relation of migration movements to average income levels in the regions is less close; most notably the regions with the highest gains from migration (the South West and East Anglia) are relatively low-income regions. The earnings of migrants in their regions of origin and destination do not seem to be representative of the general levels in those regions.

The distribution of industry in the last two or three decades has followed trends very different from those of the nineteenth century. There has been a strong tendency for industries to grow faster or decline more slowly in the regions where they are less strongly represented — in other words, diversification of regional industrial structure and dispersion of individual industries has been the tendency, rather than specialization and localization. To some extent this simply reflects the relative decline of industries that had previously become highly localized, but that accounts for only part of the trend; regional policy, too, may account for some of it. In general it seems likely, however, that the tendency is mainly due to the increasing extent to which modern manufacturing industry is 'footloose', because of the improvement of transport and communications, the changing nature of industry and the compact geography of the country. The tendency to cluster together in a central situation has been stronger recently in some service activities than in manufacturing industry proper; hence much of the continued growth of the South East. Latterly, however, market forces, together with some encouragement from policy and perhaps from faster transport and better communications, have produced a considerable dispersion of office work. This has, as yet, however, mostly been confined to within a hundred miles of London.

Regional policy, to which some passing references have already been made, is of long standing in the United Kingdom. The first manifestation of it — rather different in form from later ones — was the measure introduced in 1928 to assist movement of labour from areas of heavy unemployment to job-opportunities elsewhere. The policy was perhaps inappropriate to a period of high general unemployment and was in any case unpopular in the areas from which labour was moved; it was abandoned after a decade. Meanwhile, from 1934 other measures began to be taken to encourage movement of job-opportunities to the most depressed areas and, modest though these measures were, there were signs that they were producing some results immediately before the Second World War.

The war itself largely suspended regional differences in prosperity by producing general full employment, moving activity towards peripheral areas and stimulating some of the localized industries, for example shipbuilding, which had been in decline. However, thinking about postwar policy proceeded on the assumption that the prewar problems would return. The Barlow Report recommended government control of the location of new industrial establishments,[1] and the White Paper on employment policy gave some support to such measures.[2] Subsequently, the Town and Country Planning Act of 1947 gave the Board of Trade power to control new industrial building through the issue of Industrial Development Certificates, and the Distribution of Industry Act, operative from the previous year, gave powers for various forms of assistance — grants, loans, renting of government factories — to developments expected to create employment in the designated Development Areas.

With the assistance of some remaining wartime powers and in the presence of postwar shortages of buildings and manpower, regional policy made a powerful impact on the distribution of industry in the first five postwar years; but thereafter, with the slackening of controls and shortages, and in the absence of the expected early return of depression in the old exporting industries, its effect weakened. The recession of 1958 marked the re-emergence of the regional problem as an evident matter for concern and policy measures began to be strengthened. The greatest single strengthening came in 1963, when measures were introduced that amounted to differential assistance of something over 15 per cent

---

[1] Royal Commission on the Distribution of the Industrial Population, *Report,* Cmd 6153, London, HMSO, 1939.
[2] *Employment Policy,* Cmd 6527, London, HMSO, 1944.

to typical capital expenditure on industrial establishments in the assisted areas. The form of assistance was changed, but its cost not greatly altered, by the Act of 1966, which also redefined the Development Areas as large, coherent entities containing collectively about a fifth of the manufacturing industry of Great Britain. (The government of Northern Ireland applied parallel but somewhat stronger incentives.) In 1967 there was added the Regional Employment Premium, a subsidy amounting initially to about 7.5 per cent on manufacturing wages in the Development Areas. Two years later, following the report of the Committee on Intermediate Areas,[1] a new class of area was introduced in which benefits were available on a reduced scale. A class of Special Development Areas had already been introduced in 1967, mainly comprising districts in which coalmining employment was declining especially fast, to which certain additional assistance was given.

In 1970 the form of assistance was changed and its amount greatly reduced. The emergence of heavy and substantially localized unemployment in the following year, however, prompted the introduction in 1972 of benefits not very different in scale from those of the late 1960s — cash grants towards the cost of plant and machinery in the Development and Special Development Areas, and of buildings and works in both these and the Intermediate Areas. On a typical industrial project in the Development Areas the assistance might amount to about 19 per cent of the capital cost. At the same time Intermediate Area status was extended to the whole of the North West and Yorkshire and Humberside. Subsequently, in 1974, the Regional Employment Premium, previously condemned to expire in the autumn of that year, was reprieved, but although the rate of payment was increased, the new sums were a smaller percentage of wages than originally in 1967.

The new measures of 1972 included, however, besides these benefits which were automatic, further provisions for selective assistance to employment-creating industry by various forms of grant and loan, normally (together with the automatic benefits) not exceeding some 45 per cent of the total cost of the project for an enterprise in a Development Area. The selective benefits were made available to some mobile service establishments as well as to manufacturing industry; later, in 1973, further benefits were announced to subsidize the movement of key workers who went to assisted areas with such mobile service establishments. In August-

[1]Department of Economic Affairs, *The Intermediate Areas,* Cmnd 3998, London, HMSO, 1969.

November 1975, there was, briefly, a further subsidy to sustain employment in the assisted areas in cases where redundancy threatened, but this benefit was subsequently extended to the whole country. Later measures of regional significance have mostly taken the form of assistance to particular firms with establishments in the assisted areas. The armoury of inducements to industry to move into or expand in the assisted areas is thus now quite a formidable one. On the other hand, it must be noted that in recent years the stringency of control over industrial building by Industrial Development Certificates has been considerably relaxed, most notably by the raising of the minimum size of development for which a certificate is required.

In addition to the financial incentives and the restrictions that have been briefly described, there have been attempts at the promotion of development by the direct provision of facilities. The building of government factories to rent to industrialists in some degree at concessionary terms was one of the earliest and has been one of the continuing strands of regional policy — fairly modest in scale, but broadly successful. The building of new towns, originally conceived as a means of relieving pressure of population in the overcrowded conurbations, developed, especially in Scotland and the North, and later in central Lancashire, into an attempt to provide 'growth-points' for the economic rejuvenation of the respective regions. Additional central government assistance in the removal of industrial dereliction and the modification of the pattern of road development in the interests of areas in need of an economic stimulus have also played some part in general regional policy.

Specific measures of this kind can certainly be effective in particular cases, especially where the whole pattern of settlement in an area needs to be changed to make it suitable for modern industrial activities. But, in a closely settled industrial country with a very extensive (even though often old) urban infrastructure, the problem of renewing growth is very different from that in, for instance, a country that is bringing large rural populations into non-agricultural work. One lesson of experience in the United Kingdom seems to be that rather strong incentives, perhaps supplemented by prohibitions, are needed to direct development into regions that are physically not badly equipped to support it, but would not attract it through the working of market forces alone. Governmental opinion seems, implicitly, to have swung back to this view, after an interval in which the desirability of operating mainly through the provision of infrastructure and the establishment of growth-points was favourably considered.

In view of the determination with which some kind of regional policy has been pursued over a long period, it is important to know, if possible, how effective it has been. It is not, of course, practicable to say with confidence what would have happened in any period without any regional policy at all, the more so since there has been no period for a long time in which the effects of regional policy can be presumed to have been negligible. The latest period of strong policy, since 1972, has not yet lasted long enough for its effect to be assessed, but studies have been made of the change — assumed to be largely due to policy — between the 1950s, when policy was relatively weak, and the middle and late 1960s, when it was stronger. In this interval big changes came about both in the pattern of 'moves' (including the establishment of branches) by manufacturing industry and in the regional distribution of industrial building. Changes can also be detected in the regional distribution of employment growth when that part of it attributable to differences in regional industrial structure is eliminated.

The upshot of such studies is that, between the two decades in question, growth of employment in the assisted regions was augmented by some 30,000 or 40,000 a year in manufacturing industry, which might have been expected to bring secondary increases in employment growth ultimately building up to a further 20,000 or 30,000 a year. Bearing in mind that regional policy was by no means absent in the 1950s, it seems reasonable to suppose that the policy operated in the middle and late 1960s may have augmented employment growth in the assisted areas, in comparison with what would have happened with no policy at all, by some 70,000 to 100,000 a year. If this is accepted, it follows that, in in the absence of any regional policy, the situation of those regions would have been very markedly worse that it was. It seems likely that the excess of their unemployment rate over that in the rest of the country might have been something like twice as great as in fact it was and their net loss of population by emigration perhaps twice as great also. In that case Scotland, in particular, would have suffered an absolute fall in population, possibly of the order of 0.5 per cent a year. This has happened in the past to no British region, except briefly to Wales in the years of interwar depression. It would certainly have imposed a major strain on national unity. The situation in Northern Ireland, where the natural increase of population has become very rapid, would also have been even

27

worse than it in fact became.

What seems to emerge, then, from a consideration of the regional problems of the United Kingdom is that the relative mildness of interregional differences and migration flows has owed much not only to the compensating effects of centralized public finance and the compactness of the country, but also to specifically regional policy. Without that, the story would have been very different, politically as well as economically.

Chapter Two

THE MAIN SECTORS

1. The Industrial Sector

Industrial production

Industrial production accounts for about 45 per cent of GDP. Before the actual decline in output in 1974 and 1975, the normal pattern was that industrial production would grow slightly faster than GDP, whilst manufacturing production would, in turn, be growing rather faster than total industrial production. However, the major reason for industrial production lagging behind manufacturing has been the absolute decline in mining and quarrying. Construction has grown relatively slowly, but gas, electricity and water have been among the major growth industries. The absolute decline of the mining and quarrying sector is now being reversed as North Sea oil begins to make its impact.

Within the manufacturing sector there have been two industries which have suffered an absolute decline since the war. One is shipbuilding and marine engineering, which was at a peak in 1956 but has declined by over 20 per cent since then, although fluctuating a great deal from year to year. The other is leather and fur, which is a very small industry anyway. The associated clothing and footwear, and textile industries, although not suffering an absolute decline, have grown very slowly in the postwar period and have both shed a large number of workers. Other slow-growing industries have been metal manufacture and other metal goods. It is these industries — shipbuilding, mining, textiles, clothing and metals — which were the basis of Britain's early industrialization; now they are all of fading importance.

The food, drink and tobacco industry grew at 2.3 per cent per annum from 1955-75, but with the drink and tobacco sector expanding much faster than food. Paper, printing and publishing grew at a slightly slower rate than manufacturing, recording a 1.8 per cent growth-rate between 1955 and 1975—rather less than the 2.4 per cent for bricks, pottery, glass and cement. The other medium-growth industry has been vehicles, which grew at 3.0 per cent per annum up to 1973, although, because it was so badly hit in 1974 and 1975,

Table 2.1. *United Kingdom industrial production (output)*

	1970 weights	Annual growth-rates	
		1955-75	1965-75
		(percentages)	
Food, drink and tobacco	84	2.3	2.0
Coal and petroleum products	7	3.5	2.1
Chemicals and allied industries	58	5.5	4.5
Metal manufacture	57	−0.3	−2.7
Mechanical engineering	100	2.7	2.1
Instrument engineering	15	5.4	3.4
Electrical engineering	67	4.4	4.1
Shipbuilding and marine engineering	16	−0.4	1.4
Vehicles	73	1.1	−0.3
Other metal goods	48	0.8	−0.5
Textiles	49	0.8	0.9
Leather and fur	3	−1.2	−1.7
Clothing and footwear	24	1.0	1.0
Bricks, pottery, glass and cement	27	2.4	1.3
Timber and furniture	22	2.6	1.2
Paper, printing and publishing	64	1.8	0.6
Other manufacturing	31	4.0	2.8
Total manufacturing	745	2.3	1.5
Construction	146	1.8	0.2
Gas, electricity and water	72	4.7	4.2
Mining and quarrying	37	−2.4	−3.4
Total industrial production	1000	2.1	1.3

Source: CSO, *National Income and Expenditure* (various issues).

its growth over the period 1955-75 is barely over 1 per cent.

The engineering and allied industries have experienced a rapid growth in the postwar period. Technical developments have meant that the leading industry has been electrical engineering, with a growth-rate of 4.4 per cent per annum over the period 1955-75, compared to about 3 per cent per annum for engineering as a whole. The development of new weapons systems, the spread of new domestic appliances, the electrification of the railways, and the expansion of the Post Office's telecommunications networks have meant a substantial and continuing demand for the output of the electrical engineering industry and in particular its electronics section. Instrument engineering has been growing slightly faster, but mechanical engineering, though still the most important of the three, producing 55 per cent of engineering output, has been growing more slowly (2.7 per cent per annum between 1955 and 1975).

Technical developments have been the major factor responsible for chemicals and allied industries being the fastest growing sector in manufacturing. Plastics and similar materials have replaced metals in many uses and synthetic materials have replaced natural fibres in the textile industry and elsewhere; new products have been introduced and other products modified using chemical-based compounds. The result has been that these industries have grown at 5.5 per cent per annum in the last twenty years.

The output of coal and petroleum products has also grown exceedingly fast due to the growing demand for oil products in all walks of life. Of course the substitution of new chemical-based products for old has meant that metal manufacture, leather and fur, cotton textiles and similar industries have suffered accordingly; hence their below-average rates of growth. Metal manufacture has also been hit by the decline of its traditional user industries, such as shipbuilding, the railways, defence and heavy engineering generally.

A further industry, not so far mentioned, is other manufacturing, which has been growing at a rate of around 4 per cent per annum. This above-average growth can largely be explained by increased demand for rubber (for cars, flooring, etc.) and for plastic products not elsewhere specified, which together account for most of the output of the sector. The sector also includes toys and sports equipment, and these too, at a time of rising incomes and increasing leisure, have been growing extremely fast.

The figures for capital expenditure and employment (Table 2.2) show that, whilst manufacturing output has been growing at around 3 per cent per annum in the last twenty years, the inputs of labour and capital have grown at widely different rates. The employment figures for the period 1948-71 show that the number of workers in manufacturing has risen by only 0.6 per cent per annum on average. This is in sharp constrast to the growth in capital, which over the period 1948-68 has been at a rate of about 3.4 per cent per annum. This increase in capital has meant that labour has become more productive in most sectors. Within manufacturing, however, there have still been large differences in the growth of employment and capital in different sectors.

Table 2.2. *United Kingdom industrial production (inputs)*

	Employment		Capital	
	1975 (June) (000s)	Annual growth-rate 1948-71[a] (%)	Annual growth-rate 1948-68[b] (%)	Fixed capital formation 1968-73[c] (£m)
Food, drink and tobacco	740	1.2	4.7	250.2
Coal and petroleum products	468	1.0	5.7	103.3
Chemicals and allied industries				292.0
Metal manufacture	501	0.1	3.6	223.6
Mechanical engineering				
Instrument engineering				
Electrical engineering	2,084	1.1	3.5	395.0[d]
Shipbuilding and marine engineering				
Vehicles	759	1.0	3.3	168.0
Other metal goods	547	1.0	3.6	..[d]
Textiles	543	−1.7	−1.9	
Leather and fur	42	−1.6	1.8	158.6
Clothing and footwear	412	−0.6		
Bricks, pottery, glass and cement	284	0.1	5.2	..[e]
Timber and furniture	267	—	3.5	..[e]
Paper, printing and publishing	568	1.4	3.2	118.6
Other manufacturing	330	1.7	3.4	220.9[e]
Total manufacturing	7,545	0.6	3.4	1,930.1
Construction	1,279	0.2	n.a.	n.a.
Gas, electricity and water	355	0.7	n.a.	763.3
Mining and quarrying	355	−3.2	n.a.	170.2
Total industrial production	9,534	0.3	n.a.	n.a.

SOURCES: Department of Employment, *British Labour Statistics Yearbook,* London, HMSO (annual); R.C.O. Matthews, 'Some aspects of postwar growth in the British economy in relation to historical experience', paper read to the Manchester Statistical Society 1964, as extended by A.J. Buxton, University of Warwick.

[a]Because of the change (in 1971) from card count to Census basis, it is not possible to calculate growth-rates for employment 1948-75.

[b]Growth in the gross stock of reproducible fixed assets at constant prices.

[c]Annual average of gross fixed capital formation at 1970 prices.

[d]Other metal goods included in figure for engineering and shipbuilding.
[e]Bricks, etc. and timber and furniture included in figure for other manufacturing.

The largest increase in capital since the war has in fact been in the fastest growing sector, namely the chemical industry. There the growth in capital has been at a cumulative rate of 5.7 per cent per annum (1948-68), whilst output has grown by 6.1 per cent per annum (1951-74) over a nearly comparable period. This contrasts with the rate of growth in employment of 1.0 per cent per annum (1948-71), which itself is an above-average rate of growth. In recent years fixed captial expenditure in the chemical industry has been larger than in the whole of the engineering and shipbuilding industries, whose output is three times that of the chemical industry. This partly reflects the technical complexities of many modern chemical processes, but is also one of the reasons why the industry has expanded so fast.

In bricks, pottery, glass and cement there has also been heavy investment and capital has grown by over 5 per cent annually, with employment hardly increasing at all. Much of this investment has been in the glass industry, where the float glass process has been a major innovation.

There has been, perhaps surprisingly considering its relatively low growth-rate, substantial capital expenditure in the food, drink and tobacco industry, where capital has grown annually by 4.7 per cent between 1948 and 1968, and employment by 1.2 per cent. The development of new products, the growth of the market for frozen food and packeted convenience foods, and the rapid growth of the drink and tobacco sector have been responsible for this heavy investment.

The only manufacturing industries where there has been a decline in employment since the war are textiles, leather and clothing, where the work-force has fallen by about 500,000 — some 30 per cent. These industries have been subject to a fall in capital as well, with textiles being the worst hit of the three and clothing remaining the most buoyant. In two other industries — metal manufacture, and timber and furniture — there has been a static work-force, but in both investment has been substantial. The fastest increases in employment have come in food, drink and tobacco, paper, printing and publishing, and other manufacturing, where the work-force has been rising by 1.2 per cent, 1.4 per cent and 1.7 per cent a year respectively (1948-71), at a time when the total working population has risen hardly at all.

So far as actual numbers employed are concerned, the engineering industries still dominate manufacturing employment, with over 2 million workers (1975) out of a total of just over 7.5 million in manufacturing as a whole. There are also 760,000 in the vehicles sector and 1,050,000 in metals and other metal goods. Despite the declining work-force, textiles and clothing are still very labour-intensive and together employ some 1 million workers. The other large employing sectors are food, drink and tobacco with 740,000 workers and paper, printing and publishing, where there are 568,000 workers. Outside manufacturing, there are 1.3 million working in the construction sector, although the work-force has been growing only very slowly, and there are still over 355,000 in the mining and quarrying sector despite its rapid decline. The redeployment of miners has been a problem, because as recently as 1959 there were some 750,000 employees in the mining and quarrying sector, but ironically in the last few years the problem in the coalmines has been the failure to retain labour rather than redundancy.

There has been a relative decline in the importance of industrial employment in the total, while experience has varied considerably between different regions (see Chapter 1).

Concentration
This section gives a brief review of the recent trends in industrial concentration, both in the aggregate and in individual markets, together with a short survey of government policy towards monopoly and restrictive practices. Most studies of concentration have been concerned with possible monopoly power in the hands of private companies; consequently the nationalized enterprises, including public utilities, coalmining and, since 1968, the iron and steel industry, have been excluded. (In 1968 employment in the iron and steel industry accounted for roughly 4 per cent of the total in manufacturing industry.)

The changes in aggregate concentration, that is in the manufacturing and distribution sector as a whole, enable us to gauge the changing importance of the largest privately owned enterprises in the economy. Two estimates suggest that in the first half of this century the level of aggregate concentration increased moderately, and in fact probably fell during the decade spanning the Second World War. Measuring the relative dispersion of publicly quoted companies in manufacturing, mining and distribution, Hart and Prais found a significant increase between

1896 and 1939,[1] but by 1950 relative dispersion was little different from that at the turn of the century. Similarly, in a study of the hundred largest firms in manufacturing industry, Prais estimated that their share in the total net output of the sector rose from 16 per cent in 1909 to only 24 per cent in 1935. By 1949 the share had fallen slightly to 22 per cent.[2] It is possible that wartime planning controls ensured a larger share of output for smaller firms than would otherwise have occurred and that this helped to interrupt, in the period 1939-50, the long-term moderate rise in concentration.

Since 1950 the upward trend has not only been resumed but has shifted very markedly. According to Prais, by 1970 the hundred largest enterprises accounted for 41 per cent of the net output of the manufacturing sector.[3] As a group they have therefore nearly doubled their share in a little over twenty years. There is no simple explanation of why the rate of aggregate concentration should have accelerated so sharply, but a number of statistical analyses have established that, compared with the remarkable rise in the share of the largest *enterprises* in manufacturing net output, the share of the hundred largest *plants* (or establishments) has remained more or less unchanged at 10-12 per cent for the last forty years (the longest period for which estimates can be made). The demands of technology forcing firms to build mammoth plants in order to take advantage of production economies of scale cannot, therefore, be held responsible for the increase in the concentration of enterprises. (This is not to say, of course, that the absolute size of the largest plants has not increased.)

On the other hand, since the late 1950s and early 1960s, several studies have indicated that larger firms have been growing on average proportionately faster than smaller firms. In the first half of the century there was no such systematic tendency. An important factor that probably helps to explain this faster proportionate growth, and hence the concentration increase, is merger activity among large firms. Since the early 1960s merger have increased substantially in volume and importance, reaching a

[1] P.E. Hart and S.J. Prais, 'The analysis of business concentration: a statistical approach', *Journal of the Royal Statistical Society* (series A), vol. 119, part 2, 1956.

[2] S.J. Prais, *The Evolution of Giant Firms in Britain,* Cambridge University Press, 1976.

[3] Ibid, see Appendix A: in comparing 1949 with 1970, an adjustment to the Census statistics is necessary to ensure that the steel industry is treated comparably in both years.

peak in 1968 (when the value of acquisitions more than doubled from the previous year) and again in 1972. A detailed study of the effect of mergers on the inequality in size between manufacturing firms suggested that they probably accounted for about one-half of the observed change in the period 1954-65. In view of the considerable merger activity after 1965, subsequent analysis is likely to show it with an even more important role.

Taken together these points suggest that the accelerating increase in concentration in manufacturing has been caused by the larger firms maintaining a faster proportionate growth than smaller firms, a process assisted by widespread acquisition and resulting in a substantial rise in the number of plants operated by the largest firms.

Market concentration does not *have* to rise simply because aggregate concentration has increased. For example, the largest firms in manufacturing could increase their share of the sector's output as a whole by diversifying their activities across a wide range of markets without causing significant individual increases. In view, however, of the extent of the recent increase in aggregate concentration, such a result would be surprising, especially as it is known that the largest firms in absolute size are frequently amongst the leaders in individual markets. The measurement of market concentration can be an important first step in assessing the extent of monopoly power in individual industries, but two preliminary points should be noted. First, the level of seller concentration in a market is only one of several important characteristics of market structure which have a bearing on monopoly power. Of equal importance are, for example, the conditions of entry, the extent of product differentiation and the level of buyer concentration. Secondly, data from the Census of Production, which are frequently used to measure market concentration, suffer from a number of well documented shortcomings for the purpose in hand and these should be borne in mind when considering the results discussed below.

Detailed studies of market concentration using the material from the Census of Production have been made for 1935, 1951, 1958 and 1968. Comparisons over time of concentration levels for individual products or product groups (which we refer to as 'market concentration') meet a formidable number of problems, but the result is fairly firmly established that, on average, market concentration rose persistently over the period 1935-68. Thus the average concentration ratio for comparable sets of products or product groups increased between 1935 and 1951, between 1951 and 1958 (for a different set of products) and again between 1958 and 1968 for a sample of 150 products. By 1968 the five-firm average concentration ratio had reached just over 65 per cent.

These figures refer to the average change throughout product groups in manufacturing industry. But perhaps of more significance for the problem of monopoly power is the growing importance of very highly concentrated products — those where the five largest firms account for 80 per cent or more of total United Kingdom output. In 1958, in a sample of 214 product groups in manufacturing, about 18 per cent of sales was accounted for by groups where the five-firm concentration ratio was 80 per cent or more; the comparable figure for 1963 was 24 per cent of sales. An important increase also took place between 1963 and 1968. In a comparable sample of 288 product groups, those heavily concentrated accounted for just over 34 per cent of total sales in 1963, but for 39 per cent by 1968. By that year product groups accounting for nearly three-quarters of the sample sales had five-firm concentration ratios of 50 per cent or more, and those accounting for half of the sales had ratios of at least 70 per cent.

On the face of it these figures hint at a widespread potential for the exercise of monopoly power, either through the market share of a single dominant seller or through tacit oligopolistic price co-ordination. While the concentration figures alone are sufficient to raise important policy questions, it must be stressed that they provide only a first step in the full analysis of market structure, which ideally reqtires a detailed case-study approach.[1] But analysis has shown that for manufacturing industry as a whole, and indeed for broad industrial groups within manufacturing, mergers played an important part in the increase in concentration observed over the period 1954-65, although the level of industry aggregation was too wide to assess the effect of mergers on market concentration. Clearly, if a large number of mergers were 'conglomerate', as many are in the United States, their effect on market concentration would have been neutral.

To overcome this difficulty, an intensive study of a random sample of thirty product groups was made for the period 1958-63. The results suggested that out of the twenty-one groups where

---

[1] Apart from the qualifications already made above, it is also important to note that Census of Production data refer only to United Kingdom output and hence ignore an important source of competition in many cases, namely from imports.

concentration increased, in ten it could be attributed to mergers, while in eleven it was due essentially to the internal growth of the leading firms. Again it should be noted that this inquiry stopped before the peak of merger activity in the latter part of the 1960s, and there are some indications that a follow-up study for later years would show a more significant role for mergers even at this level of industry aggregation. The statistics thus suggest that market concentration has been increasing persistently in recent years, and that a large number of individual product groups are now very heavily concentrated.

British policy towards competition and monopoly entered a new phase in 1973 with the passing of the Fair Trading Act, which created the position of Director General of Fair Trading, with overall responsibility for co-ordinating policy on competition and consumer affairs through the new Office of Fair Trading. To appreciate more fully the scope of that office we sketch below the main elements of British policy since 1948.

Until the creation of the Monopolies Commission in 1948,[1] there was no modern law which sought to regulate or control possible abuses of market power. In that year the Monopolies Commission was empowered, at the direction of the Board of Trade, to investigate how 'the public interest' was affected in industries where one firm or a group of firms acting together controlled one-third or more of the United Kingdom market. There was no presumption in its inquiries against large market shares or in favour of competition and the definition of what constituted 'the public interest' was left deliberately vague and largely up to the Commission to decide. Its reports presented a detailed historical and contemporary analysis of the industries investigated, with, if necessary, recommendations to Parliament as to how the public interest could be better served in the future. Most of its earlier reports were concerned with cartels rather than individual positions of dominance. It was the knowledge gained in these inquiries of the particularly damaging effects on actual or potential competition that could follow the close regulation by restrictive agreements among producers of prices, outputs, discounts, authorized dealers and other matters that led to the next stage of British policy. The Monopolies Commission had

---

[1] Over the years the title of the Commission has changed. Originally it was the Monopolies and Restrictive Practices Commission, in 1956 it became the Monopolies Commission and in 1973 the Monopolies and Mergers Commission. For convenience we refer to it throughout as the Monopolies Commission.

performed the valuable service of making public the extent and probable effects of a wide range of restrictive practices; the subsequent task was to ensure that any abuses were corrected.

The 1956 Restrictive Trade Practices Act provided for the registration of all restrictive agreements and their scrutiny by the specially constituted Restrictive Practices Court. The register, which is open to public inspection, was maintained by the new Registrar of Restrictive Agreements. In two important aspects this section of the 1956 Act marked a new departure: first, the fact that a Court could hear cases of this kind was a 'revolutionary step in British constitutional law and procedure'; secondly, the restrictive agreements were deemed to be against the public interest unless the Court was convinced otherwise on one or more of a number of grounds laid down in the Act. The grounds are that: (a) it protects the public from injury; (b) the public derives a benefit from it; (c) it offsets the restrictive practice of another firm or trade association; (d) it enables producers to negotiate fair terms with a monopoly buyer; (e) employment *or* (f) exports would suffer if it were abandoned; (g) it maintains another restriction upheld by the Court. If the Court accepts the argument for the maintenance of the restriction on one or more of these grounds, it then has to be satisfied that the restriction is not unreasonable having regard to the balance between these circumstances and any detriment to the public or to persons not parties to the agreement. Thus, there is a general presumption in favour of competition except where this is rebutted. In 1964 the practice of resale price maintenance was brought within a similar procedure under the Resale Prices Act.

On the face of it the success of the 1956 Act appears to have been remarkable. By the middle of 1972, for example, a total of 2,620 registrable agreements had been ended, or modified so as not to infringe the Act. Similarly resale price maintenance had been almost universally abandoned. But, as overt (and registrable) agreements were ended, there was growing concern about the use of 'information' agreements, which did not formally come within the machinery of the 1956 Act, but which might enable firms to achieve the same degree of collusion. Consequently an attempt was made in 1968, in a further Restrictive Practices Act, to bring such agreements within the scope of the Court by providing for the registration and possible scrutiny of certain classes of such agreements. In the view of the authors of a recent study of the effects of the restrictive practices legislation, as far as information agreements were concerned 'the 1968 Act seems to have delivered the final *coup de grâce;* by this time it seemed evident that generally industry had decided to drop what remained [of their restrictions] rather than register'.[1]

For a period in the late 1950s and early 1960s the control of restrictive practices rather overshadowed the residual tasks of the Monopolies Commission in examining positions of market dominance. However the increase in merger activity in the 1960s, noted above, rapidly produced a major policy response. In 1965, the Monopolies and Mergers Act empowered the Board of Trade (now the Department of Prices and Consumer Protection) to refer to the Monopolies Commission for investigation mergers which involved the creation or increase of a market share in the United Kingdom of at least a third, or where the assets acquired were valued at £5 million or more. There were special provisions for mergers involving newspapers. At the end of its inquiries (which normally can last up to six months) the Commission has to recommend whether or not the merger is likely to operate against the public interest. If the conclusion is that the merger is likely so to operate, the Board of Trade has the power to prevent the merger, to unscramble it if it has already taken place, or to allow it to proceed subject to conditions.

Just as the major emphasis of British policy was at one time on the control of restrictive practices, it is probably true to say that now the major concern is with the behaviour and performance of dominant firms and the emergence or strengthening of positions of dominance by merger.

The whole basis of British policy has been placed on a firmer foundation by the 1973 Fair Trading Act, which supersedes the previous legislation in this field and brings the several strands of policy together under the authority of the Director General of Fair Trading. His department has become the focal point for the collection of information and the initiation of action. Thus he now has power to make references on monopolies to the Monopolies Commission. The scope for inquiry by the Monopolies Commission has been widened in several ways under the 1973 Act: for example, firms having 25 per cent of the United Kingdom (or local) market can now be referred, also nationalized enterprises; restrictive agreements relating to services have to be registered and may be the subject of a case in the Restrictive Practices Court. The Director General of Fair Trading is chairman of the committee

[1]D. Swann, D. P. O'Brien, W. P. Maunder and W. S. Howe, *Competition in British Industry,* London, Allen and Unwin, 1974, p.163.

that decides which mergers to recommend for reference to the Monopolies Commission and he assumes full responsibility for proceedings under the Restrictive Practices Acts. Thus, 'for the first time, the implementation of the monopolies and restrictive practices legislation will be brought together, so that the Director General should be able to take a more comprehensive view of the working of competition in the economy than either the Department of Trade and Industry or the Registrar have been able to do in the past'.[1]

2. The Services Sector

Britain, like the United States before it and others besides, is nowadays becoming a service economy. The distinction between 'goods' and 'services' is not sharply defined. Should transportation be regarded as an integral part of goods production or as a service? The repair of a pair of shoes undertaken on the premises of a retail establishment would count as a service, but if the shoes were sent back to the manufacturer the repair would probably count as goods. Nevertheless, a rough division of industries is illuminating. Leaving aside agriculture, which in Britain is in any case small, we classify as 'goods industries' mining, manufacturing and construction, and then treat all the rest as services. On this basis 13.5 million people were employed in services and 9.2 million in goods in the United Kingdom in 1975. If we were to transfer transport and communications to the goods side, however, the service sector would be only slightly larger than the goods sector. Moreover, the figures here refer to employees in paid employment and exclude self-employed persons. The use of Census of Population data would raise a little the share of services in total manpower, but a slightly different picture again would be given if output were used rather than employment or manpower as the measure.

As a rule there is wider fluctuation in goods employment than in services, a difference especially marked in the interwar period. This fact, combined with the shadowy nature of the line separating goods from services,[2] makes it difficult to discern trends, but it

---

[1]E. L. Smith, 'The Fair Trading Act', *Trade and Industry,* 9 August 1973, p.304.

[2]In the reclassification of manpower which took place in 1959, 700,000 men who had been listed under manufacturing under the old Standard Industrial Classification of 1948 were transferred to distribution.

appears that in the United Kingdom there was a tendency for service employment to grow faster than goods employment in the interwar years, a tendency reversed by the war, when the distributive trades especially lost a substantial part of their manpower to the armed forces and war production. Since the war, and especially since the 1950s, the comparatively faster growth of service employment has been renewed. In the most recent period in fact service employment has continued to rise, while goods employment has actually been falling. In Table 2.3 we show the industries here classed as services, with the employment in them for two recent years, 1969 and 1975, and the change between those years. At the foot of the table we give the total of goods employment, that is in mining and quarrying, manufacturing and construction, in the same two years.

The recent rise in employment in insurance and banking and in catering and hotels draws attention to another way of looking at the importance of services in the economy. In 1975 visible exports were valued at £18.8 billion; in the same year credits for sea and air transport, travel and other private services were £7 billion; that is Britain earned abroad over a third as much by selling services as

Tables 2.3. *United Kingdom employment in service industries compared with total in goods industries, 1969 and 1975*

| | Employees | | Change |
| | 1969 | 1975 | 1969-75 |
	(thousands)		(%)
Gas, electricity and water	406	353	−13.1
Transport and communications	1,561	1,518	−2.8
Distributive trades	2,711	2,763	+1.9
Insurance, banking and finance	893	1,103	+24.0
Professional and scientific services	2,849	3,556	+24.8
Catering and hotels	710	826	+16.3
Miscellaneous services	1,284	1,376	+7.2
Government service			
National	598	650	+10.9
Local	867	1,005	+15.9
Total in service industries	11,879	13,150	+10.7
Total in goods industries[a]	10,249	9,156	−10.7

SOURCE: CSO, *Annual Abstract of Statistics, 1976,* Table 149.
[a]Mining and quarrying, manufacturing and construction.

by selling goods. On the other hand, the expenditure on private services of £5.5 billion was only a quarter of the outlay on visible imports of over £22 billion. There is in fact normally a substantial surplus on invisible account (which includes other items as well as services) to offset the deficit on visible account. The earnings of financial institutions, commonly called 'the City', are of particular interest. Total credits from private services were £6.2 billion in 1974, and insurance, banking, merchant banking and brokerage brought in about 10 per cent of this. If we take both sides of the account, credits and debits together, there was a net surplus on account of private services of £1.2 billion. The net earnings of the City as a whole, taking into account not only the proceeds from services currently performed, but also the earnings from overseas investments, came to £900 million.

The reasons for the comparative growth of service employment in advanced countries are well known. As a rule, rising real income leads to a disproportionate rise in the demand for services. Moreover, over long periods the manpower requirements for given outputs tend to fall more slowly in services than in manufacturing. There are plenty of exceptions to this, and there is also a tendency for services previously marketed to be replaced by self-service, as a result of which part of service output may be taken out of the national accounts. On balance, service employment is likely to rise in relation to goods employment even faster than the relative rise in output. Income elasticities are obviously a strong factor in explaining the growth of service employment, but there have been complementary explanations, for example, that the structure of markets is more conducive to restrictive practices in service trades, which are thus less competitive and less prone to introduce labour-saving advances, although, of course, it is not easy to see how the labour 'productivity' of such services as hairdressing or grave-digging can easily be improved.

The measurement of output and productivity in service industries is notoriously difficult. John Gorman has shown, for instance, that if the business of banks is regarded as the production of money for people to hold, then, in the United States over the period 1948 to 1966, measured productivity was *declining* at annual average rate of 1.5 per cent; whereas if one takes the view that the banks' primary business is the facilitation of spending, then measured productivity has been *increasing* at an annual average rate of 2.75 per cent.[1]

[1]Victor R. Fuchs (ed.), *Production and Productivity in the Service Industries,* New York, Columbia University Press, 1969.

Table 2.4. *Annual average changes in productivity, 1951-66*

Percentages

Goods industries		Service industries	
Mining	1.6	Transport	2.9
Food, drink and tobacco	1.9	Gas, electricity, water	4.4
Chemicals	4.8	Distribution	2.5
Metals	2.1	Finance	1.3
Engineering	2.5	Professional services	0.4
Textiles	2.8	Miscellaneous services	2.3
Other manufacturing	2.7	Public administration	0.8
Construction	1.6		

SOURCE: A.D. Smith, *The Measurement and Interpretation of Service Output Changes,* London, National Economic Development Office, 1972.

Different methods of calculating productivity change yield varying results, but they all tend to show a slower trend in the increase of labour productivity in most service trades than in goods. A similar difference has been noted in the United States, Canada and elsewhere.

A. D. Smith gives estimates of annual average changes in labour productivity over the period 1951-66 (Table 2.4). British indirect taxation has traditionally fallen on commodities, especially because purchase tax, introduced during the Second World War and continued since, fell mainly upon manufactured goods. Until 1966 very little indirect taxation fell upon services. This bias against manufactures was partially redressed by the introduction in 1966 of the selective employment tax, a tax on employment in certain service trades. This imposed on employers in some industries a tax of a certain amount per week for each person they employed, varying according to whether the worker was adult or juvenile, male or female. The administration was somewhat complicated in as much as the amount of the tax was added to the weekly National Insurance contribution paid by all employers for all employees irrespective of their trade, but then employers in defined industries were allowed a refund (initially with a premium in the case of manufacturing). The initial tax was fairly low and as a proportion of costs could not be said to redress fully the bias against manufactures in the system of indirect taxation. The rate was raised subsequently, before the whole tax was abolished and replaced in 1973 with value-added tax (VAT), which also replaced purchase tax on goods.

Besides securing a broader base for indirect taxation other merits were claimed for selective employment tax. In particular it was suggested that it would offset alleged tendencies to waste labour in some service industries. This question, among others, was exhaustively analysed in two extensive research reports undertaken on behalf of the government by Professor W. B. Reddaway and associates at the Department of Applied Economics in Cambridge. The first report on the distributive trades was published in 1970 and concluded that productivity in the distributive trades had risen significantly more after 1966 than could have been expected on the basis of earlier relationships between employment and the volume of sales in retailing and the pressure of demand for labour. It could not be concluded that the whole of this exceptional rise in productivity was the result of selective employment tax, since at about the same time the abolition of resale price maintenance had come into force and economic reasoning would lead one to expect such a measure to increase the productivity of labour in industries affected. In the final report Professor Reddaway maintained that the evidence was statistically very weak in industries other than distribution, but he personally found 'the evidence for a modest productivity gain moderately persuasive'. These conclusions command fairly general acceptance, though some question has been raised concerning the *scale* of the productivity improvement in distribution which could be attributed to selective employment tax and the abolition of resale price maintenance, it being suggested that certain other factors common to all industries, including manufacturing, might also have played a role.

An incidental conclusion of the study as it referred to the distributive trades was that the imposition of this particular kind of indirect tax had rather a small effect on gross retail margins (inclusive of tax), thus making selective employment tax an exception to the fairly general rule that a substantial part of indirect taxes is passed on to the final consumer.

3. The Agricultural Sector

Proportionately fewer people are engaged in agriculture in Britain than in any other country of any size—2.7 per cent of the civil working population—but virtually all suitable land not built upon by towns and cities is in agricultural use, and the sector provides just over a half of the country's food requirements, or two-thirds of all that can be grown in temperate climates. Britain has been a net importer of food since the middle of the nineteenth century, but the share of home production in total supplies reached a low point between the two wars and has lately been rising a little.

There are over 270,000 farming units in Britain, but of these two-fifths are very small, mostly farmed part-time, and account for less than 4 per cent of the industry's output. Of the 170,000 full-time businesses, one-fifth are large (employing four or more men) and between them produce more than half the total output. The average size of full-time holdings is 259 acres (105 hectares).

British agriculture is highly specialized and highly capitalized. Three-fifths of full-time farms are devoted to dairying, beef cattle and sheep, a sixth are crop farms and the remainder specialize in pigs, poultry, or horticulture, or they are mixed farms. There is also specialization according to region; for example, arable crops are mainly grown in eastern counties.

The composition of British farm production has not changed a great deal in recent years, as shown in Table 2.5. The principal crops are wheat, barley and potatoes, and the principal livestock products are milk and milk products, which constitute between them over a fifth of total agricultural output.

The total area of land in agricultural use in the early 1960s was the same as in the 1930s, but in the past decade the acreage has diminished by over 3 per cent, partly because of incursions of urban development. Output in real terms is nearly three times that achieved before the war. The proportion of land given to farm crops has risen somewhat, so that the average yield per acre of the principal crops, such as wheat and barley, has about doubled.

Table 2.5. *Distribution of agricultural output,[a] 1964-5 and 1975-6*

Percentages

	1964-5	*1975-6*
Farm crops	19.9	22.7
Horticulture	11.6	10.7
Livestock	35.7	38.4
Livestock products	32.1	27.6
Total of above	99.3	99.4

SOURCE: CSO, *Annual Abstract of Statistics, 1976,* Table 245.
[a] In value terms.

More than half of British farms are owned by their occupiers, the remainder being farmed by tenants of private landlords. In the latter cases the capital equipment required to operate the farms is most commonly provided by the tenants. Production methods are highly mechanized: there are nearly five tractors to every six people engaged in the industry and, at one tractor to every 32 acres of arable land (13 hectares), Britain has one of the highest tractor-densities in the world.

From the middle of the nineteenth century until the third decade of the present century Britain followed a policy of free trade in goods and services, including food. This meant that, when great advances were made in transport and refrigeration, the British consumer had access to the cheapest food supplies throughout the world. When Britain abandoned free trade in 1932, tariffs were introduced on most imported foodstuffs, with zero or preferential rates for Commonwealth countries. The intention was not primarily to protect British farmers, but to give a trading advantage to exporters in the British colonies and dominions. Since, however, a great many of the preferences were fixed in specific rather than *ad valorem* terms, the value of this concession to Commonwealth suppliers has diminished as prices have risen. Nonetheless, some degree of preference was available to them on 90 to 95 per cent of United Kingdom 1972 imports of food, drink and tobacco, oilseeds and vegetable oils. During the Second World War there was an intensive campaign for the development of British home food supplies and imported supplies came under very close government control, which was gradually relaxed in the postwar period. Since 1 February 1973, Britain has begun to take part in the EEC Common Agricultural Policy (CAP).

In 1961 two-fifths of British food imports came from Commonwealth countries, a quarter from Western Europe and 13.5 per cent from North America. In the 1960s the Commonwealth share was slowly falling and the West European share rising. Since 1972 the EEC the share has risen strongly (see Table 2.6).

For over half a century the size of the British agricultural industry was largely determined by market forces—by the ability of British farmers to compete with overseas suppliers—but in the First World War and again in the Second overseas supplies were drastically curtailed by submarine warfare. Between the wars a variety of forms of agricultural support were introduced. These were, of course, enormously intensified during the Second World War, and subsequently a higher degree of State support remained

Table 2.6. *Food imports by area of origin, 1972-5*

Percentages

	1972	1973	1974	1975
EEC	31.0	35.1	44.0	49.1
Rest of Western Europe	6.9	7.1	6.5	5.2
North America	11.6	12.0	10.9	8.2
Rest of World	50.5	45.8	38.6	37.5

SOURCE: CSO, *Annual Abstract of Statistics, 1976.*

than had existed previously. Most industrial countries give State support to agriculture, but in the majority of cases this takes the form of tariffs and/or quantitative restrictions, including outright prohibition of certain imports. Until joining the EEC British policy was quite different. The price paid by British consumers for food in the shops was based on the world price, that is the price of the cheapest import.[1] The British farmer, however, was given a guaranteed price for major products other than fruit and vegetables. The difference between this guaranteed price and the market price was made up by a 'deficiency payment' financed by the State. In addition there were specific production grants and subsidies. The guaranteed price and production subsidies were calculated in such a way as to secure for the farmer a reasonable income, as well as a surplus to finance the capital requirements of the industry.

Because of the increasing budgetary cost of this system some additional protective measures were introduced in the 1960s designed to reduce the volume of cheap food imports and hence to maintain United Kingdom market prices. The most important were the introduction of minimum import prices and import levies on major cereals and later on beef and veal, negotiation of quotas on

[1]During, and for nearly a decade after, the Second World War, the prices of many foods, whether imported or home produced, were kept down by consumer subsidies. When these were abandoned, various forms of 'agricultural' or production subsidies remained. Consumer food subsidies were re-introduced by the Labour Government of 1974, and in 1974-5 amounted to £652 million. Under the plans contained in the Treasury White Paper of February 1976 (*Public Expenditure to 1979-80,* Cmnd 6393) they are to be phased out once more—a mere £50 million being put down for 1979-80.

pigmeat imports and the introduction of an import duty on mutton and lamb, previously duty-free. Thus, even before joining the EEC, Britain was moving towards a system that was in many respects similar to the CAP, while maintaining the subsidy to farm incomes given via the guaranteed price system and production grants.

The effects of British entry into the EEC in 1973 may be considered from the point of view of farmers, consumers and overseas suppliers. It was generally expected that farmers would be least affected; total farm income rose a fraction more than average between 1972 and 1975. Farmers continue to enjoy protection; competition from other Community members is limited to the extent that there is a common price throughout the area, so that transport costs give natural protection to the local industry; protection from non-Community suppliers is given by the levies imposed on imports from outside. The exact amount of gain or loss for any particular farmer depends on the type of farming.

For the British consumer it may be expected that the price of food relative to other products will rise. Entry into the EEC has coincided with an enormous increase in world food prices, so that it is hard to say of any particular food price increase how much was owed to the change in world prices and how much to the CAP. The effect of the CAP has since become more marked.

The effect on overseas suppliers is of course to switch towards supplies from other members of the Community and away from previous suppliers. The most notably affected is New Zealand, over a third of whose exports have until lately come to the United Kingdom. The other principal group affected is the cane sugar suppliers covered by the Commonwealth Sugar Agreement. But the final effect of the CAP on British agriculture cannot be determined until the long-term relationship between food prices in the EEC and the world has become clear. If the former tend to stay above the latter, then the farmer will, in general, benefit at the expense of the rest of the population, and vice versa.

Most commodities are now supported by the mechanisms of CAP, which are administered by the Intervention Board for Agricultural Produce. Expenditure in the United Kingdom under CAP regulations was about £300 million in 1975-6, of which more than three-quarters was reimbursed by the European Agricultural Guidance and Guarantee Fund.

Chapter Three

SOCIAL ISSUES

1. Trade Unions and Labour Relations

Structure and organization

In 1975 the number of workers in the United Kingdom who were members of trade unions was estimated at 11,950,000.[1] This represents 51 per cent of the working population (excluding employers, self-employed and members of the forces). Male membership was 8,508,000 and female membership 3,442,000, so that 60 per cent of male workers and 37 per cent of female were members of unions. The number of unions operating in the United Kingdom was estimated at 488 in 1975 and this total has shown a steady decline over the years, from 630 in 1965 and from 688 in 1955. Total membership of trade unions has risen slowly throughout the century with no large movements in either direction; in 1945 membership was 7,875,000.[2] The rising number of members coupled with the falling number of unions has meant an increase in their average size. This has occurred both through internal growth and through amalgamations. The largest unions in the United Kingdom at present are the Transport and General Workers Union with a 1975 membership of 1,857,308, the Amalgamated Union of Engineering Workers with 1,300,477, and the General and Municipal Workers Union with 883,810.[3]

The great majority of unions in the United Kingdom are affiliated to the Trades Union Congress (TUC), which has its headquarters in London. In 1975 the TUC had an affiliated membership of 10,584,393. Similar bodies exist in Northern Ireland and Scotland, but many unions which represent members in these areas are in any case affiliated to the TUC.

Unions in the United Kingdom have developed in the main along

---

[1] *Department of Employment Gazette,* November 1976.

[2] Department of Employment, *British Labour Statistics: historical abstract 1886-1968,* London, HMSO, 1971.

[3] TUC, *Report of the 107th Annual Congress, 1975,* Blackpool.

craft lines, except in the case of general unions which recruit from a wide variety of workers. Craft unions are those to which workers with a particular skill, craft or training belong, regardless of the industry in which they are employed; electricians in all industries will tend to be in one union, as will engineers. Whereas general unions have usually catered for less skilled occupations, craft unions predominate in trades or professions requiring significant levels of skill and/or training. This form of union organization along craft lines contrasts with the industrial union, under which workers of many different skills will be in a single union relevant to the industry in which they are employed. Industrial unions are common in some European countries, for example West Germany. They are not found in the United Kingdom, although in the mining industry the National Union of Mineworkers comes close to the pattern, representing as it does the industrial interests of the vast majority of workers in the industry. More usually the role of bargaining agent at the industry level is filled by a confederation of trade unions. In construction, for example, there is the National Federation of Building Trades Operatives, which operates at industry level.

Unions in the United Kingdom are normally governed by an executive council, which is elected from and by the membership of the union, either directly or through an annual delegate conference. The majority of unions have a full-time staff headed by a General Secretary, who is the national spokesman for the union and its main adminstrator. Most sizeable unions also appoint full-time paid local officials to deal with union business at a local level. In almost all cases unions have an organization of lay members at local and regional level. Union members as a rule belong to a group at their place of work, but are also likely to be members of a union branch in the geographical location of their work—a branch which includes members from other work-places in the area. The union group in the work-place usually elects a spokesman, often called a shop steward. Where there are several unions involved in an establishment, there is commonly a committee consisting of shop stewards from each union, and this body is frequently an important negotiating agent with management.

Trade union objectives

Trade unions exist to act in the interest of their members; in general this has been seen in practice in terms of maintaining and improving the terms and conditions of employment for various

51

groups within the union, although unions frequently assist individual members in cases such as claims for industrial injuries compensation and claims alleging unfair dismissal. Apart from these individual cases, some of the more important matters on which unions negotiate include pay, hours of work, working conditions, industrial health and safety, fringe benefits, pensions and redundancy arrangements. Popularly, pay is perhaps the most obvious single concern of union members, and the role of unions is sometimes discussed solely in relation to pay, but other matters pursued by unions in attempting to improve their members' terms and conditions of employment are of considerable importance and should not overlooked.

The organization of workers into craft unions has implications for collective bargaining on many of the issues mentioned in the previous paragraph, because unions will often seek to negotiate national agreements which set minimum standards for rates of pay, hours of work, holidays, overtime and other premium payments, recruitment and apprenticeship. These minimum standards provide a base, and workers at the plant or company level can then negotiate individual additions to the agreed national minima. This may lead to differences between rates of pay at the place of work and those agreed nationally.

In pursuit of their various objectives, unions are often parties to procedures which have been agreed with management to regulate the conduct of negotiations or the settlement of a grievance. In the event of negotiations being unsuccessful the union may resort to direct action in support of its case. Direct action can vary through several types of non-cooperation to a complete withdrawal of labour — a strike. Industrial action may occur before all procedures have been exhausted and may be undertaken by a particular group of local union members without prior permission of the executive council of their union or unions. If action continues without such sanction it is called unofficial. Action which has been approved by the national union organization, or which has started and subsequently received such backing, is termed official action. Many unions pay strike pay to members engaged in official withdrawals of labour.

Trade unions and the government

Trades unions, employers' associations and the general field of labour relations are the responsibility of the Department of Employment, formerly the Ministry of Labour. Before the 1960s the role of the Ministry of Labour was to assist in the orderly running of the system of industrial relations in the United Kingdom, with little reference to or interest in the subject or outcome of particular disputes. For many years the Ministry offered facilities for conciliation and arbitration in the event of a dispute and the Minister had the power to establish a Court of Inquiry into a particular dispute if it was considered necessary.

This form of *ad hoc* arrangement was, in the main, satisfactory as long as unions and employers were engaged in a process of free collective bargaining at either national or local level. In the 1960s, however, increasing government concern with inflation and the subsequent development of incomes policies, wage restraint and other anti-inflation instruments has meant that the government is no longer content to leave unions and employers to negotiate freely. The government is now more interested and involved in the outcome of collectively bargained decisions and much more concerned with industrial disputes in the course of such bargaining. The government, central and local, is a very large employer in its own right, and this provides another incentive for its growing involvement with industrial relations.

As a consequence, the trade union movement, through the TUC, and the main employers, through the Confederation of British Industry (CBI), are now frequently consulted by governments on the formulation of policies, particularly those concerned with inflation. Representatives of both bodies sit on the National Economic Development Council, which is chaired by the Chancellor of the Exchequer. The Conservative government in 1972 consulted extensively with both bodies in the formulation of its counter-inflation policy, and the Labour government which assumed office in 1974 made their understanding with the TUC, the 'social contract', an important feature of their economic strategy. Consultation with the TUC and the CBI took place before the government introduced from July 1975 a twelve-month limit on wage rises of £6 a week, and before a second stage of wage restraint was introduced from the following July.

Trade unions and the law

Apart from consultation over policy, governments in recent years have been closely involved with changes in the legal framework regulating trade union conduct and organization. In 1964 a Royal Commission was set up under Lord Donovan to review the current state of trade unions and employers' organizations; the Labour government received its report in 1968.[1] Although the Labour Party traditionally has been closely linked to the trade union movement and has drawn much support from it, in the aftermath of the report the government introduced proposals for legislation to curb what was seen as a major problem of unofficial or unconstitutional strikes.[2] The action proposed was stronger than that recommended by the report and the TUC was strongly opposed to the penal sanctions contained in the proposals. The government subsequently abandoned their attempts to legislate, relying instead on the TUC's undertaking to implement a programme of action giving Congress more power to involve themselves in unofficial strikes and inter-union disputes. The other move following the Donovan Report was the establishment of a standing Commission on Industrial Relations (CIR), which was to examine problems concerning recognition by employers of trade unions and other industrial relations issues.

The Conservative government which came into office in 1970 passed in 1971 a wide-ranging Industrial Relations Act. This established a new branch of the High Court, the National Industrial Relations Court (NIRC). The Court was empowered to sit in judgement over what were called cases of 'unfair industrial practices' if one of the parties brought a case and could impose fines if breaches of the law occurred. The NIRC could also impose a full ballot of union members, or a 'cooling-off' period to postpone a planned industrial action if the government made an application.

The opposition of the trade union movement and the Labour Party to the Industrial Relations Act led to considerable controversy over the decisions of the NIRC and, when Labour was elected to office in February 1974, repeal of the Industrial Relations Act was given high priority. The Trade Union and Labour Relations Act 1974 abolished the NIRC and the CIR, and in general restored the situation broadly to a pre-1971 state, although retaining greater protection against unfair dismissal.

Further employment measures were enacted or came into force during 1975. The Equal Pay Act 1970 became operative in December 1975, having given employers a transitional period of

---

[1]Royal Commission on Trade Unions and Employers' Associations, *Report,* Cmnd 3623, London, HMSO, 1968.

[2]Department of Employment and Productivity, *In Place of Strife: a policy for industrial relations,* Cmnd 3888, London, HMSO, 1969.

five years to meet its requirements. The Sex Discrimination Act 1975 makes illegal discrimination on grounds of sex or marriage in many fields including employment and training. The Employment Protection Act 1975 extends the rights of employees regarding unfair dismissal and discrimination short of dismissal because of union membership. It institutes new procedures for handling redundancy situations and provides in certain circumstances for guarantees of pay by an employer when he is unable to provide work for reasons other than a trade dispute.

The Act also established on a statutory basis the Advisory, Conciliation and Arbitration Service (ACAS), which was first set up in September 1974. ACAS has taken over and extended the role previously filled by the Department of Employment in providing conciliation in industrial disputes and union recognition problems, arbitration and mediation. The emphasis is on a voluntary solution to industrial relations problems and ACAS has to be approached by at least one of the parties to a dispute before becoming involved, although it can inquire into any situation and offer advice independently. The body is independent of government and controlled by a representative council.

2. Social Policy

For at least a century there has been a secular trend for a higher proportion of both national resources and public expenditure to be devoted to social services. Even before the First World War, the idea was emerging that social services should not be regarded as a form of charity, but rather as one of the natural benefits available to the citizens of a civilized State. Stimulated by both world wars, the State increased its powers and pushed ahead with the development of social services. But it was not until after the Second World War that the services became comprehensive. The broad pattern of the social services as they are at present was laid down in the 1940s, but they have not remained static, and developments in the last thirty years have aimed at continued improvement in the levels of services and more satisfactory administration to cope with rising needs. Table 3.1 shows public expenditure on the social services and housing in recent years as a percentage of gross domestic product at factor cost.

Health and welfare services
The National Health Service was set up in 1948 to promote the provision of comprehensive health treatment available according to

55

Table 3.1. *Public expenditure[a] on the social services and housing (at current prices), 1951-75*

	1951	1961	1971	1975
	(£ millions)			
Education	433	1,012	3,023	6,840
Health and welfare services	564	1,088	2,785	6,707
Social security benefits	707	1,628	4,309	8,918
Housing	367	555	1,253	4,291
Total	2,071	4,283	11,370	26,756
	(percentages)			
As a proportion of GDP	*16.4*	*17.7*	*23.3*	*28.7*

SOURCE: CSO, *National Income and Expenditure* (various issues).
[a] Current and capital expenditure and grants by public authorities and public corporations.

medical need without regard to any insurance qualification. It was originally free to users, but various charges have subsequently been introduced from time to time. The aim of policy has been to meet needs for cure and rehabilitation, to prevent illness and to promote health. The methods by which these aims were pursued have been an increase in personnel, better training and research, greater integration of services, and the renewal and modernization of the hospitals.

Between 1951 and 1975 the medical and nursing staff in the hospitals almost doubled, and other professional and technical staff trebled. The number of general medical practitioners increased much more slowly — by only about 30 per cent over the same period — while the number of dentists rose by about a fifth.

The trend in health administration, particularly over the last decade, has been towards greater integration of the services provided by hospitals, general practitioners and local authorities. This has been particularly evident in the treatment of children, the elderly, the mentally ill and the mentally handicapped. There has been increased emphasis on rehabilitation to reduce the length of stay in hospital and to return patients to their own homes as soon as possible, with continued treatment when necessary at out-patient clinics or in day hospitals. As a result, the average length of stay in hospitals generally has decreased sharply, at the same time as the number of patients treated both as in-patients and as out-patients has risen rapidly. Moreover, much of the treatment was in more modern hospitals, as the government embarked on a programme of rehabilitation and, where necessary, rebuilding.

Although there are only indirect indicators of progress in health services, they suggest striking improvements in standards of physical health in the last twenty years. The main infectious diseases, which were once the major cause of death of people of working age, have been virtually eliminated as health problems. People in Britain live longer than in most other countries; the proportion of children who die in the first year of life is among the lowest of all countries in the world. There has been a steady increase in sickness and death from degenerative diseases, largely attributable to the ageing of the population. Part of the increased cost of the health service is due to changes in the age structure, but a major part is due to technological changes — the use of new drugs, new diagnostic tests and new treatment in virtually every field of medicine.

Education

Between 1951 and 1975 public expenditure on education at constant prices increased nearly three times. As a proportion of gross national product it has risen steadily from 3.4 per cent in 1951 to 7.3 per cent in 1975. This reflects a considerable increase in the numbers in full-time education, both at schools and at universities and colleges of further education. The growth has been uneven, reflecting the fluctuating birth rates since the war.

The school-leaving age was raised to 15 in 1947 and to 16 in 1973. In addition a decreasing proportion of pupils leave school at the first opportunity; instead they stay on voluntarily. As a result, by 1975 there were 50 per cent more pupils at school than in 1951. The increase in the number of children has been more than proportionately matched by increased numbers of teachers. In the public sector, where more than 90 per cent of all children receive their education, many more pupils are now taught in comprehensive schools. There has been a massive school building programme in the last thirty years and, although there are still a number of unsatisfactory schools, particularly in urban areas, a large proportion of children are now educated in modern schools.

The increase in numbers of pupils staying on at school has also been reflected in an improvement in standards in the school-leaving examinations and an increasing proportion of school leavers now move into full-time further education.

A ten-year education programme was announced by the government in December 1972. The proposals involved substantially increased expenditure in five sectors: a new programme of nursery education; a larger building programme for the renewal of secondary and special as well as primary schools; a larger teaching force to improve further the staffing standards in schools; new measures to improve the pre-service and in-service training of teachers; and the development in higher education of a wider range of opportunities for both students and institutions.

Income support

The system of income support consists of many elements, but the central one is the social security system. Social security payments increased from 5.5 per cent of personal income in 1951 to 11.6 per cent in 1975. More than half of this increase was due to higher expenditure on retirement pensions.

The main purposes of the social security system are to replace earnings in periods of interruption or cessation of earnings, and to transfer extra income to those who currently have family responsibilities. This involves a redistribution between those in good health and the sick, between the working population and the unemployed and retired, and between those currently with family responsibilities and those without.

The postwar National Insurance scheme created rights to benefits which are taking years to mature, before the whole population over pension age can draw pensions earned by contributions under the scheme, or all widows, long-term sick and work-injured can receive benefits on the new basis. Thus the cost of social security has been increasing because the postwar scheme is still maturing. In addition, a number of changes in policy since it was introduced, such as the family income supplement, have added to the cost.

Between 1951 and 1975 total expenditure on retirement pensions at constant prices increased more than fourfold, although the population of pension age increased by only 40 per cent. But the proportion of the population of pension age actually receiving pensions increased from 60 per cent in 1951 to 88 per cent in 1975. This is mainly because a higher proportion of pensioners had had time to pay contributions from 1948 onwards which gave them title to pensions, but there has also been a trend towards earlier retirement.

The rates of both absence through sickness and unemployment are also higher now than in the 1950s. A large increase in sickness absence in the 1960s has been almost entirely due to increases in incapacity rates at all ages. The reasons for this trend are complex and it is not confined to Britain.

Between 1951 and 1975 the population under 21 increased by nearly 20 per cent, but children for whom family allowances were paid increased more — by 40 per cent. This was partly because the number of families with two or more dependent children increased more than the number of children, and partly because an increasing number of children stayed on at school after the age of 15 and continued to be counted for purposes of family allowances

For all these reasons social security expenditure has been increasing within the framework of the 1945-6 legislation quite apart from changes in policy. In addition benefits have been increased, not just in line with changes in prices, but with the object of improving their real value. Improvements have taken the form of supplements related to earnings and increases in the real value of basic flat-rate benefits and allowances. A further policy aim has been to ensure that those entitled to benefits and allowances actually claim them.

A further part of income support is the supplementary benefits scheme, which in 1966 succeeded national assistance. Every person aged 16 or over who is not in full-time work, attending school or involved in a pay dispute and whose resources are insufficient to meet his requirements is entitled to a supplementary benefit. In 1948 11.5 per cent of persons over pension age were drawing national assistance; in 1975 18 per cent were drawing supplementary benefits.

Housing
Satisfactory housing implies adequate numbers of dwellings of the right size and quality in the right places. There are nearly 20 million dwellings in Britain and nationally the numbers of households and dwellings are about equal, but they are unevenly distributed and housing shortages persist in the more prosperous commercial and industrial centres, such as London and Birmingham.

Over 8 million new dwellings have been built in Britain since 1945 and two families in five now live in a postwar dwelling. During the past thirty years the demolition of slum dwellings and higher standards for new housebuilding have led to significant improvements in the general quality of British housing. However, there remain a large number of older dwellings, some of which have been kept in good repair and modernized, while many others are unsatisfactory by modern standards. A sample survey in 1971 showed that 12 per cent of dwellings lacked an internal water closet and 7 per cent were regarded as unfit.

The number of people owning their own homes has increased rapidly in the last fifty years, until over half of all dwellings are owned by their occupiers. Some 30 per cent are rented from public housing authorities and most of the remainder are rented from private landlords. A national system of rent rebate and allowance schemes has been introduced to assist poorer tenants. The main objectives of government housing policy are to secure decent homes for every family, to offer families a fairer choice between owning a home and renting one, and to ensure fairness between one citizen and another in giving and receiving help towards housing costs. Government subsidies are available for local authorities which incur financial debts in clearing slums and providing adequate public sector housing in areas of housing shortage. Another major objective has been to enable more people with moderate means to become owner-occupiers.

Nevertheless, a satisfactory housing policy has proved difficult to achieve. Rent control has led to many anomalies and the rapid move to owner-occupation has caused big increases in house prices and a shortage of mortgage funds. Moreover, sharp changes in policy have resulted from changes in governments and there have been wide variations in the resources devoted to housing investment. A housing policy which will achieve the objectives described above has yet to be evolved.

Chapter Four

PUBLIC FINANCE AND NATIONALIZED INDUSTRIES

1. Changing Patterns of Public Expenditure

Although adjustments to the level of public expenditure have never usurped the role of taxation changes as the principal means of short-term economic regulation, it is difficult to over-estimate the significance of public sector demand both to the growth and full utilization of resources in the long term, and to the short-term stabilization of demand. Since 1961, with the publication of the Plowden Report on the *Control of Public Expenditure,* it has been an established axiom of policy that the growth of public sector demand in aggregate should be decided by reference to the 'prospective development of income and economic resources', the measure of which is taken as the secular growth-rate of GDP. Under this system, the objective of policy is to balance public sector and other claims on resources (consumption, private investment and exports) in the medium term (of five years), so that the need for short-term interventions is minimized, both with respect to the necessity for correcting destabilizing fluctuations in public expenditure itself, and with respect to counter-cyclical demand operations. Because of the high degree of inflexibility in public programmes such interventions can prove costly. However, although this strategy has always allowed for modest changes in public spending where cyclical conditions warrant it, calls made on the instrument have tended to increase. Since 1973-4 changes in expenditure plans have been much larger than previously envisaged.

Most of the characteristics of public sector demand in the 1960s and 1970s have been determined by successive medium-term strategies, operating through the Public Expenditure Survey Committee (PESC), established in 1961. From 1962 to 1967 public expenditure plans were framed around the National Economic Development Committee and the National Plan growth exercises. The annual public expenditure White Papers, which have been published regularly since 1969, have been prepared against less

Table 4.1. *Public expenditure in the United Kingdom as a proportion of GDP at factor cost, 1955-75*

Percentages

	1955	1960	1965	1970	1975
Public authorities' expenditure[a]					
Goods and services					
Consumption	18.9	18.8	19.4	21.0	24.6
Capital formation	3.8	3.7	4.8	5.7	5.3
Total	22.7	22.6	24.2	26.7	29.9
Transfers	9.8	9.9	11.3	14.4	16.8
Debt interest	4.6	4.5	4.3	4.7	4.2
Expenditure, excluding debt interest, by function					
Defence	9.1	7.2	6.8	5.7	5.6
Social services excluding education	10.1	11.0	12.6	14.8	16.8
Education	3.3	4.1	5.1	6.1	7.3
Housing	2.6	1.7	2.3	2.5	3.8
Other	7.3	8.5	8.8	12.0	13.2
Total expenditure, excluding debt interest, by spending authority					
Central government					
Goods and services	14.4	13.7	13.4	13.9	15.4
Transfers	9.2	9.6	10.7	13.6	15.6
Total	23.6	23.4	24.1	27.6	31.0
Local authorities					
Goods and services	8.4	8.4	10.8	12.8	14.5
Transfers	0.6	0.6	0.6	0.7	1.2
Total	8.9	9.1	11.4	13.5	15.7
Total public authorities' expenditure[a]					
Excluding debt interest	32.4	32.5	35.6	41.1	46.7
Including debt interest	37.0	37.0	39.9	45.8	51.0
Public corporations' expenditure[b]	4.4	4.0	4.4	4.2	5.4
Net lending	0.7	0.6	1.0	0.6	2.1
Total public sector expenditure[c]	42.1	41.6	45.3	50.6	58.5
Total public sector resource share[d]	35.4	34.9	38.1	40.8	49.2
of which:					
Direct claims	25.5	24.6	26.7	28.1	32.6
Indirect claims	9.9	10.3	11.4	12.7	16.6

SOURCES: CSO, *National Income and Expenditure* (various issues); NIESR estimates.

*a*Excluding net lending.

*b*Capital expenditure on fixed assets plus increases in the value of stocks, net of capital transfers from the public authorities, and debt interest paid other than to the public authorities.

*c*National accounts definition, which differs from the White Paper definition by including imputed rents, all nationalized industries' investment and a gross estimate of debt interest.

*d*See text: equivalent to demand on national output, as defined, for instance, in Treasury, *Public Expenditure to 1979-80,* Table 4.2. On this definition expenditure is net of (i) investment grants, (ii) imputed rents, (iii) indirect taxes on public sector transactions and intra-sector subsidies, (iv) direct taxes on transfers and debt interest, (v) net lending and net purchases of land and existing buildings and (vi) the estimated savings by the recipients of transfers and debt interest.

optimistic projections of available resources, though with changing ideas of the proportion of such resources which the public sector should pre-empt.

The development of public expenditure as a percentage of GDP through the 1950s and the first half of the 1960s has been examined by the Musgraves,[1] and Table 4.1 carries this analysis through to 1975. The expenditure breakdown is confined to the central and local governments (public authorities), but the (mainly capital) expenditure of the public corporations is added to the table, together with net lending, in order to indicate the total size of the public sector as it is defined in the national accounts.[2] The table also categorizes expenditure on an economic basis, distinguishing current from capital expenditures, and direct expenditures on goods and services from transfers, in the form of subsidies and grants to the personal and overseas sectors, and from interest payments in respect of the national debt. Expenditures are also sub-divided on a functional basis, distinguishing them by main head of programme.

While the total of public expenditure is important for the financing requirement, and therefore for monetary policy, about one-fifth does not constitute a demand on production, because one

[1]R. A. and P. B. Musgrave, 'Fiscal Policy', in R. E. Caves *et al., Britain's Economic Prospects,* Washington DC, The Brookings Institution, 1968.

[2]As from 1976-7 investment by the nationalized industries is included in the White Paper definition of public spending only if it is financed by government loans.

has to allow for items which are purchases of existing assets (real and financial) and for the taxes and subsidies paid on the government's own purchases (which actually appear on the revenue side of the public sector accounts). As far as indirect expenditures are concerned, account is also taken of the element which comes back to the government in direct taxes, and the proportion which will be saved by the recipients rather than added to the total of national expenditure. An estimate of the public sector 'resource' share calculated in this manner is therefore given in the table in order to make the total of public sector demands directly comparable with national output.[1] It is, in fact, such an estimate of public demand on resources, rather than gross expenditures, which is the strategic element in planning expenditure growth against prospective GDP growth. It is customary, also, to distinguish direct claims (a large proportion of which is made up of the wages and salaries of public employees) from indirect claims, which constitute transfers from one sector of the population to another.

The Musgraves noted that the public authority expenditure ratio had declined somewhat during the 1950s, but had risen substantially during the first half of the 1960s, reaching the level of 40 per cent by 1966. From 1952 the room for the growth in social and welfare expenditure, the expanding elements in GDP, was provided by the decline in defence expenditure and by a preference for private rather than public dwellings investment. With the assumption of high growth targets from the end of 1962, however, public expenditure embarked on a significant expansion, which raised its share of GDP substantially, partly because public demand achieved the targets set for it, while the other components of demand and GDP as a whole did not. By 1967 total gross public sector expenditure had reached 50 per cent of GDP from a figure of 42 per cent in 1960, which (reduced to claims on domestic product at factor cost) represented an increase in the total resource share from 35 per cent to 41.5 per cent. The reaction which followed devaluation brought the proportion down to about 40 per cent, and this pause lasted until the end of 1971, when significant changes were made in public programmes in order to combat unemployment. It was, however, from the end of 1973 that public expenditure once more took off. In 1974 the public sector pre-empted 46 per cent of GDP,

[1]See footnote *d* to Table 4.1. A fuller definition of this concept may be found in Treasury, *Public Expenditure White Papers: handbook on methodology*, London, HMSO, 1972, Chapter V.

rising to about 49 per cent in 1975-6, partly because of the recession. The cut-backs announced in 1975 and 1976 have since aimed at reducing this proportion to below 45 per cent (provided a fuller level of employment can be attained).

Nearly all sectors of public demand have shared in this overall expansion, though some programmes have been more consistent than others. Housing investment, for instance, underwent a particularly strong expansion between 1962 and 1967, and then suffered an almost equally strong reaction until 1972. The priority given to this sector in the last two years of the period, together with the large increases in housing subsidies in 1974, restored its position as the fastest growing element over the period as a whole. Education, on the other hand, was the most consistently fast-growing sector until it began to lose impetus from 1972 with inflation and revised ideas about future needs. The National Health Service has also demanded an increasing share of resources, while the opposite is true of defence, which actually underwent a decline in volume terms, as well as a drastic fall in its share of total expenditures.

A corollary of all this has been that the local authority sector, which, although it does not necessarily initiate the policies, is responsible for most expenditure on housing and education, has expanded faster than the central govenment sector as far as goods and services are concerned. Until the housing upsurge of 1973-4 this has been expressed more in current than capital expenditures. Central government investment on such projects as roads, hospitals and industrial regeneration was itself extremely buoyant up to 1973, and one has also to remember that local authority environ-mental investment was, from July 1965 to the end of the 1960s, a favourite target for short-term cuts.

On central government account, also, there have been a number of fast-expanding programmes based on transfer payments, only a small element of which is administered locally. From 1960 to 1975 the share of transfers in GDP increased from 9.9 per cent to 16.8 per cent, with the increases concentrated particularly on the years 1965 to 1968, and on the period 1972 to 1974; in 1974 alone the share rose by 2 percentage points. The expansion of the transfer element in public expenditures can be traced to reasons of both social and economic policy, with social security benefits represen-ting the means of redistributing income and the medium of reflation, as in the period 1972-4. Subsidies combine both these uses with the further one of combating inflation. The remarkable

65

rise in subsidies between 1972 and 1974 began with compensation for price restraint in the nationalized industries, and was followed, in 1974, by large increases in food and housing subsidies.

With all this, total indirect claims on resources have consistently expanded faster than total direct claims. While the proportion of GDP directly pre-empted by the public sector expanded from 25.5 per cent in 1955 to 32.6 per cent in 1975, the transfer element in public spending increased from 9.9 to 16.6 per cent. While public services have expanded in terms of employment and other purchases, it is in the transfer of purchasing power between income groups that one finds the strongest evidence of an impulse towards an increasing ratio of taxation to national income.

2. Taxation

The United Kingdom tax structure incorporates a wide range of taxes, duties and other claims on personal and corporate incomes, on expenditure on goods and services, on property and on transfers of wealth, parallels for which may be found in many Western economies. OECD statistics suggest a ratio of tax (including social security contributions) to GNP in the United Kingdom similar to the average for the other eight members of the Community. The United Kingdom ratio has been rising, particularly in the late 1960s, with that for other EEC countries relatively static (see Table 4.2). However, there are many striking differences; in particular, the United Kingdom places considerably greater emphasis on the taxation of personal incomes, while indirect taxation has traditionally concentrated on a narrow range of consumer goods, of which durables, tobacco, alcoholic drink and petroleum have been subject to particularly high rates.

Two main trends emerge when we examine the changes in the composition of tax revenues from 1960 to 1975 shown in Table 4.2. First, from 1960 to 1970 there was an increase of more than 7 percentage points in the ratio of total revenue to GNP, an expansion which coincided with the growth of public sector expenditure, with lags of a year or so due to demand conditions. The share of taxation in personal income, for instance, was fairly constant during the 1950s and up to 1963. From 1964 to 1969, however, there were large increases in the tax burden and, by the end of this period, this went to reduce the public sector deficit rather than to pay for extra public expenditure. The incoming

Conservative administration in 1970 adopted the policy of reducing taxation, so that the ratio of tax revenue to GNP fell somewhat in the period 1970-4 in response to discretionary tax cuts. This only went about half way to restoring the position of the early 1960s, and the ratio rose again in 1975 and (probably) in 1976. Much of the increase in the ratio of tax to GNP was financed through the built-in buoyancy of the personal income tax ('fiscal drag'). Over the period this provided the authorities with the means of increasing the proportion of income tax in GNP from 7.7 to 14.1 per cent. Up to 1963-4 discretionary tax cuts offset this automatic effect, but this was not true of the 1964-5 to 1970-1 Budgets.

Table 4.2. *Tax revenue in the United Kingdom and the EEC as a proportion of GNP (at market prices)*

Percentages

| | United Kingdom | | | | EEC[a] | |
	1960	1965	1970	1975	1965	1974
Taxes on all goods and services[b]	9.7	10.1	10.9	9.3	11.2	9.3
General consumption	2.0	1.8	2.5	3.5	4.8	5.3
Specific goods and services	7.2	7.6	7.4	5.1	5.8	3.6
Other	0.5	0.7	0.9	0.7	0.5	0.4
Income and profits tax[c]	10.6	11.2	15.0	16.0	8.8	11.0
Personal incomes	7.7	9.4	11.7	14.1	6.8	8.8
Corporate incomes	2.9	1.8	3.3	1.9	2.1	2.2
Social security contributions	3.5	4.7	5.2	6.6	9.1	10.8
Other taxes[d]	4.3	4.5	6.3	4.4	3.1	2.0
Total tax revenue						
Including social security contributions	28.1	30.5	37.4	36.3	32.2	33.1
Excluding social security contributions	24.6	25.8	32.2	29.7	23.1	22.3

SOURCES: OECD, *Revenue Statistics of the OECD Member Countries, 1965-74*, Paris, 1976; CSO, *National Income and Expenditure* (various issues).

[a]Average of Community of nine.

[b]Purchase tax, value-added tax, other customs and excise duties and motor vehicle licence duties, less export rebates.

[c]Taxes on income, including personal income tax, surtax and corporation tax, and on capital gains, paid by the personal and corporate sectors. Corporate sector includes public corporations and non-residents.

[d]Includes local authority rates, selective employment tax, stamp duties, death duties and betterment levy.

However, the cuts of the following three years did more than offset the effect of fiscal drag, which was itself accelerating with inflation.

On indirect tax there tends to be a less than proportional response of revenue to inflation because of the specific nature of excise duties. The history of goods and services taxation is therefore the opposite of that of the income tax. Discretionary increases have been necessary in order to counteract automatic decreases in real yield. Thus the net burden was almost the same at the end of the period as at the beginning. As a result the share of these taxes in total revenue declined from 40 per cent in 1960 to less than one-third by 1975.

In addition to the predominant role in counter-cyclical policy and demand management played by the tax system (particularly through changes in investment incentives, in personal income tax rates and allowances, and in the rates of indirect taxes governed by the regulator) the period has witnessed a series of major structural reforms. These were designed for a variety of secular objectives: to simplify the tax structure, to increase capacity and channel resources to more productive uses, to encourage growth and investment, to attain a more equal distribution of resources and other social objectives and, more recently, to co-ordinate United Kingdom fiscal structures and practices more closely with those of other EEC members. The following is a summary of the most significant of these changes.

Corporate taxation

Three major phases in the pattern of corporate taxation may be distinguished during the period. First, from 1958 to 1965 companies were subject both to a uniform profits tax and, in addition, income tax at the standard rate was chargeable on both retained and distributed profits. However, the income tax on distributions was treated as a withholding tax, creditable by the shareholder against the tax liability on his dividend income. In 1965 the uniform profits tax was renamed the corporation tax and the rate increased from 15 to 40 per cent, while, to encourage companies to 'plough back profits for expansion', the income tax on retentions was abolished. Finally, in 1973, after considerable debate about whether the pre-1965 system should be re-established, a new system based on the French 'imputation' method was introduced, under which a single rate of corporation tax was maintained, but the additional layer of income tax on distributions was abolished. Instead, companies paying a distribution become liable to an advance payment of corporation tax and the shareholder is imputed with a corresponding tax credit, which is sufficient exactly to offset his charge to income tax at the basis rate. The main argument for the 1973 reform, namely that, by removing the discrimination against distributions, greater freedom of capital movements both domestically and across international frontiers would be achieved, is reflected in the decision of the EEC Commission that the British imputation method should become the model for company taxation in the Community.

To encourage productive investment, successive governments have introduced a multiplicity of measures designed to provide financial incentives for fixed investment. For most of the period incentives were provided through capital allowances designed to provide relief from tax in respect of outlays on plant and machinery, industrial buildings and certain other qualifying capital assets; a system of accelerated depreciation operated through a combination of initial (first-year) and investment allowances, which varied both regionally and for different types of asset. Between 1966 and 1970, however, a system of cash grants to manufacturing, construction and extractive industries replaced the investment and initial allowances. The reversal of the grants policy in 1970 led to a rationalization and simplification of the pre-1966 system of accelerated depreciation, and important changes announced in the 1972 Budget included the introduction of a 100 per cent first-year allowance for all capital expenditure on plant and machinery throughout the United Kingdom.

Selective employment tax
Selective employment tax was in operation for eight years from 1965 to 1973; it was designed to serve a number of purposes, including the raising of additional revenue and the broadening of the base of indirect taxation to include services. In addition, it sought to provide assistance to the manufacturing sector, both to strengthen exports and to generate economic growth, while also encouraging increased efficiency in services by raising relative labour costs. To achieve these objectives the tax was imposed on the employment of labour, refunds being provided to manufacturing industries. Initially, a slight subsidy was also given to employment in manufacturing through excess refunds and, although this subsidy was soon discontinued, provision for paying excess refunds to Development Areas was retained in the form of the Regional Employment Premium. Selective employment tax met with considerable criticism from the outset not only for technical reasons but on basic

economic grounds. The tax was not 'a particularly satisfactory method of taxing services and, given the low rates at which it was levied, the size of any resulting shift of labour to manufacturing was questioned. More fundamentally, it seems extremely dubious in retrospect whether the choice of tax base was appropriate; the continuing poor performance of British manufacturing does not suggest that labour shortage was the main impediment to improved growth and export performance.

Value-added tax

In April 1973, purchase tax, selective employment tax and part of the customs and excise duties on tobacco and alcoholic drinks were replaced by VAT. The new tax was intended to create 'a more broadly-based structure which, by discriminating less between different types of goods and services, would reduce the distortion of consumer choice'.[1] The establishment of VAT was central to EEC policy. The principal feature of the new tax was that for the first time in the United Kingdom it extended sales taxation to a wide range of service sectors, most notably the retail trade, but, to prevent the changeover having a regressive impact, large areas of essential expenditure which have by tradition been free of any direct imposition of tax (particularly food, fuel and power, public transport and housing) were relieved of VAT through exemption or zero rating. Despite a broadening of the base of the tax in the 1974 Budget, its effective coverage remains less than 60 per cent of consumers' expenditure, as compared with the 80-90 per cent envisaged by the EEC's proposed common system. The single rate of VAT was also quickly abandoned (in July 1974); a higher rate being introduced initially on petrol only, but from May 1975 on a wide range of 'luxury' goods.

Personal income and capital taxation

Before the fiscal year 1973-4 an individual could be liable both to income tax at a standard rate and (if his income exceeded a certain amount) to surtax levied at differential rates which increased progressively with the amount of taxable income. In 1973 this dual system was replaced by a single unified tax, under which a broad band of income became taxable at a basic rate, with successive slices above this level being chargeable at graduated higher rates. At the same time the complicated system of allowances was greatly

[1]Treasury, *Value-added Tax,* Cmnd 4621, London, HMSO, 1971.

simplified. Earned income relief was abolished, but the value of personal reliefs was adjusted upwards so as to maintain their value in relation to earned income.

The 1962 Finance Act subjected speculative gains on a wide range of property and asset holdings to income tax and, where applicable, to surtax or profits tax. Following their victory in the 1964 election, the Labour government announced that a comprehensive capital gains tax would be introduced, and the subsequent legislation in 1965 provided for the separate taxation of short-term gains (taxable at an individual's marginal rate of income tax and surtax) and long-term gains (taxable at a special rate). Subsequent amendments have resolved some of the anomalies and difficulties of the original legislation, have somewhat widened the range of asset holdings subject to exemption and have abolished the short-term tax.

In October 1972 the Conservative government issued a discussion document which contained plans for the introduction of a form of negative income tax as a means of unifying the systems of personal income taxation and of income maintenance.[1] This was followed by a report from a House of Commons Select Committee, but the present Labour government has announced that it does not intend to proceed with the scheme. The government has, however, taken steps to widen the scope of capital taxation. In August 1974, a White Paper outlined the structure of a new capital transfer tax designed to block the most obvious loopholes in the existing estate duty.[2] The tax was introduced with the 1975 Finance Act. A Green Paper discussion outline of a comprehensive annual wealth tax has also been published,[3] but a Parliamentary Select Committee failed to produce an agreed majority report and legislation is likely to be delayed.

North Sea oil and gas taxation

The 1975 Oil Taxation Act established a special system of taxation for the oil and gas produced from the United Kingdom's own resources, mainly from the North Sea fields discovered in recent years on the continental shelf. The major feature of the new system is the Petroleum Revenue Tax (PRT) which had been proposed by the Chancellor during his 1974 autumn Budget speech. The rate of

[1]Treasury, *Proposals for a Tax-credit System,* Cmnd 5116, London, HMSO, 1972.
[2]Treasury, *Capital Transfer Tax,* Cmnd 5705, London, HMSO, 1974.
[3]Treasury, *Wealth Tax,* Cmnd 5704, London, HMSO, 1974.

PRT has been set at 45 per cent and the tax is chargeable on profits assessed on a field-by-field basis. Licence royalties, operating costs (excluding interest payments) and capital expenditure ('uplifted' by 75 per cent) are allowed against it. In addition to PRT, companies are liable to pay royalties at 12.5 per cent of the well-head value of oil and gas, and corporation tax at the standard rate on net revenue after deduction of royalties, PRT and expenses computed according to normal corporation tax rules. Safeguards have been introduced to protect investment by small companies and in marginal fields.

While it is difficult to calculate the income that the government is likely to derive from the North Sea, it is intended that the combined take of PRT, corporation tax and royalties should amount on average to about 55-70 per cent of net gas and oil revenues (after depreciation). The Department of Energy estimates that by the early 1980s receipts from oil and gas could be £4¼ billion at 1976 prices and exchange rates; if the relative oil price falls or the exchange rate rises revenues could be much lower.

3. Nationalized Industries

A number of basic industries, fuel and power (other than petroleum), transport and communication, and iron and steel were taken into government ownership in the late 1940s. Steel was denationalized in 1954 and renationalized in 1965. The nationalization of these basic industries was a major political transformation, the result of forces which had been developing over many years.

Since nationalization each industry has had its own special problems. In some these were created by strongly increasing demand, while in others, particularly coal and the railways, the problem was falling demand. But there were also common problems associated with the role of the industries in the economy and their relations with the government and Parliament.

The government's objectives were set out in the nationalization Statutes: first, the Boards which were set up to run the industries had a duty to raise revenues that, taking one year with another, would be not less than sufficient to meet all items properly chargeable to revenue; secondly, the industries were to be operated in the public interest. Boards were made responsible to Parliament for the overall financial position of the industries, while ministers were given powers to control investment and borrowing.

Dissatisfaction with the conduct of the industries in the 1950s, both inside and outside Parliament, led to the setting up of a Select Committee on the nationalized industries, which proceeded to a series of investigations into each undertaking. At about the same time the industries were required to borrow from the Treasury rather than on the market as had been the practice.

During the 1960s there were two White Papers on the financial and economic obligations of the nationalized industries, which attempted to set out new guidelines for their operation.[1] The 1961 White Paper emphasized that, although the industries had obligations of a national and non-commercial kind, they were not and ought not to be regarded as social services absolved from economic and social justification. It went on to note that some Boards were not making large enough provisions to cover the replacement cost of assets having regard to inflation and to provide against obsolescence. It noted the low returns obtained by some industries and pointed out that as a consequence the nationalized industries depended heavily on the savings of others to finance their investment. The White Paper explained how the Statutes should be interpreted with the aim of encouraging the Boards to increase revenue and prevent poor performance.

Following the publication of this White Paper specific financial objectives were set up for most of the industries for periods of up to five years, but the financial performance of the industries showed little improvement during the early 1960s. There was some increase in their gross trading surpluses in 1962 and 1963, but by 1964 the borrowing requirement was again rising rapidly.

The unsatisfactory position led to a further White Paper in 1967. This started from the position that the industries should be operated basically as commercial concerns and have the objectives of promoting an efficient allocation and use of resources. It laid down guiding principles for price policy and investment decisions; the technique of discounted cash flows was to be used for all important projects in the investment programmes. In addition to recovering accounting costs, prices were to be reasonably related to long-run marginal costs. Critical attention was to be paid to

---

[1]Treasury; *The Financial and Economic Obligations of the Nationalized Industries,* Cmnd 1337, London, HMSO, 1961; *Nationalized Industries: a review of economic and financial objectives,* Cmnd 3437, London, HMSO, 1967.

reducing costs and there was to be a continuous drive to increase efficiency and productivity. The system of financial targets would continue but should be interpreted more flexibly. All major price increases should be referred to the National Board for Prices and Incomes, which was also given powers to inquire into the efficiency of the industries when proposals for price increases were referred to it.

In the years following the 1967 White Paper the investment criteria came increasingly to be adopted as a useful discipline. But there were major difficulties in applying marginal-cost pricing. There was, however, a trend towards the application of more complex tariffs designed to reflect the costs of peak demand, so that time-differentiated tariffs are now used for electricity, telephones, railways and airlines, although differential charging is not carried to the optimal solution in marginal-cost pricing. In the coal industry and on the railways the application of the new criteria was especially difficult. In the coal industry the main problem was that of insuring the progression to a smaller efficient industry and the elimination of some pits which were losing heavily. The declining demand for railway transport meant that the railways Board could not eliminate its deficit by raising charges; the best it found it could do was to try to keep charges in line with general inflation. Where new investment was involved, it was, as a rule, only undertaken when the demand permitted charges which would cover costs.

The financial performance of the industries improved somewhat during the late 1960s, but conflicts with national economic policy led to a deterioration at the end of the decade. Prices and incomes policies were intensified and the industries were forced to delay price increases in line with price restraint. In mid-1974 the government attempted to reduce the nationalized industries' losses by permitting some large increases in the prices of electricity and coal, and in railway fares and telephone charges.

There were also broad government objectives relating to transport policy and fuel policy which sometimes conflicted with the main financial objectives. For example, it was argued that prudence dictated the maintenance of the coal industry in view of the uncertainty about supplies and costs of imported fuels. Similarly, a consideration of future transport needs implied that an efficient railway system would be needed, even though commercial operation in the 1960s would not have sustained the railways as a going concern. An uncontrolled run-down of the coal industry and the closure of some railway lines would also have conflicted with the government's regional policy.

Chapter Five

FINANCIAL INSTITUTIONS AND MONETARY POLICY

In the first part of this chapter, the different types of financial institutions in the United Kingdom are examined, together with their interactions and their roles in providing finance for investment, the government and individuals. Rapid developments, however, are taking place in the structure of such institutions and any summary such as this must be static. It is likely that in five years' time the picture will be as different and the present picture is from that of ten years ago. The second part of the chapter consists of a description of monetary policy and the mechanisms by which it is administered.

1. Financial Institutions

The Bank of England
The Bank of England has been in public ownership since 1946 and fulfils the functions of a central bank, including the provision of economic and financial advice to the government. For accounting purposes its business is divided into an Issue Department, which deals with the issue of notes backed by government securities, and a Banking Department, which offers banking services to the government, the deposit banks, about ninety foreign governments and international bodies, and a very small number of private customers.

As the government's banker the Bank handles the sale of Treasury bills to the public and the financial sector according to short-term financing requirements. To ensure a steady market it acts as lender of last resort to the discount houses. It also administers monetary policy by its dealing in the market for government stocks, by the use of the minimum lending rate and by regulating financial instituitons. The Bank also administers the exchange control regulations and manages the Exchange Equalization Account which holds the official reserves.

The deposit institutions

The deposit institutions are the most important part of the private sector in terms of size, numbers and lending. There are various different types.

The deposit banks consist of the London and Scottish clearing banks, the Northern Ireland banks and the Banking Department of the Bank of England. The largest part of this group is dominated by the four big London clearing banks — Barclays, Lloyds, the Midland and the National Westminster. They have thousands of branches throughout the country and handle a large number of small accounts. Current accounts on which cheques are drawn and cleared in a central clearing system are repayable on demand and carry no interest. Interest-bearing deposit accounts in theory require short notice of withdrawal, but in practice small sums are payable on demand.

A unique feature of their lending is the system of overdrafts, whereby customers are allowed to draw more than they have in their accounts up to an agreed limit and only pay interest on the daily balance outstanding. For personal customers, the tendency in recent years, however, has been towards fixed-term personal loans rather than the revolving credit of the overdraft system.

At the beginning of the 1960s the deposit banks dominated the banking sector in terms of both deposit and advances, but their relative importance has declined in recent years. Formerly they alone were subject to severe controls as to the form of their assets and their activities, but since the new system of regulations came into force in 1971, treating all banks alike, they have begun to move into areas such as the inter-bank market, which were formerly the sole province of the secondary banks.

Secondary banks include a number of different banking groups largely based in the City of London — the merchant banks, branches of foreign banks, branches of British banks mainly operating overseas and specialized subsidiaries of the clearing banks. They offer specialized financial services to companies, often launching share issues, and operate extensively in the 'parallel' money markets which grew up during the 1960s — local authority loans, certificates of deposit, inter-bank lending and the Eurodollar market — where interest rates are usually higher than in the 'traditional' money markets, such as that in Treasury bills.

Table 5.1 shows the relative importance of the deposit banks and secondary banks in the banking sector since 1969, with the figures for 1963 to show the rapid growth in the importance of the

Table 5.1. *Deposit and secondary bank shares[a] in total banking sector deposits and advances, 1963-74*

Percentages

	1963	1969	1970	1971	1972	1974
Deposits						
Deposit banks	74	43	40	38	36	27
Secondary banks	25	57	60	60	63	71
Advances						
Deposit banks	66	30	27	26	26	25
Secondary banks	33	70	73	74	72	74

SOURCE: *Bank of England Quarterly Bulletin.*

[a] At end December, excluding the National Giro and discount houses.

secondary banking sector. This took place during the period when severe restrictions were placed on the deposit banks.

Discount houses provide a mechanism for the orderly flow of short-term funds. The banks deposit money at call with the discount houses in order to earn interest on their surplus cash. The discount houses then buy short-term assets — until recently mostly 'traditional' assets such as Treasury and commercial bills, but now a wider range including Eurodollars and certificates of deposit.

The discount houses have a joint agreement to buy the whole of each week's Treasury bill issue (or that part which is left after higher bidders have been satisfied). They then pass it on to other institutions, mainly the deposit banks. In return the Bank of England will always lend cash to the discount houses in the last resort. This can occur when they do not have sufficient cash to cover the Treasury bill issue or the banks call in their deposits. Such loans are usually for one week at the minimum lending rate, although they can be at higher rates for shorter periods.

Finance houses provide instalment credit, usually in the form of hire purchase, but increasingly in the form of personal loans, to individuals and companies wishing to buy consumer durables or plant and machinery. Their main sources of funds are deposits from the secondary banks and overdrafts from the clearing banks, although some of the larger houses have branches which accept deposits from individuals.

The National Giro was founded by the government in 1968 and

operates through the Post Office. It provides an inexpensive cheque account and money transfer service for individuals and companies. In conjunction with a finance house it has now moved into the field of personal loans. Legislation is now before Parliament to enable the National Giro to provide the full range of lending services.

There are over 400 building societies, ranging in size from the large national societies to one-branch institutions. They are outside the normal sphere of financial control as they are regulated by the Registrar of Friendly Societies as non-profit organizations. Their purpose is to lend money on mortgages to owner-occupiers for house purchase and they obtain their funds from individuals in much the same way as savings banks. Ordinary depositors receive a lower rate of interest than shareholders, but have additional security in the event of liquidation. There are also added incentives for regular savers and all savers get priority over non-savers in mortgage lending. The authorities can take, and have taken in the past, steps to ensure that the building societies are able to compete successfully for deposits with the banks by limiting the interest payable on small bank deposit accounts.

Other financial institutions
Insurance companies and pension funds use the funds they receive as premiums and pension contributions mainly to buy long-term assets — company securities, government bonds and property; they are also important buyers of new share issues. In addition they do a relatively small amount of loan and mortgage business. As the size of their funds, particularly pension funds, grows, their position and power in the stock market become increasingly important.

There are also two principal types of collective investment institutions — investment trusts and unit trusts — whose assets are shares in other companies, usually public and quoted on the Stock Exchange. Shares in investment trusts are themselves traded on the Stock Exchange, whereas 'units' in a unit trust, which can be compared with the American mutual fund, are bought and sold at a price calculated to reflect the value of the assets, and declared by the managers, usually daily. Over the past decade there has been a rapid growth in the market share of unit trusts, but they still represent a very small proportion of the whole market in equities.

Special investment agencies have been established since 1945 to provide medium- and long-term capital to companies which have difficulty raising it from other sources. The most important are the Finance Corporation for Industry and the Industrial and

Commercial Finance Corporation Limited. The former lends sums of over £200,000 for the re-equipment and development of industry. The latter offers financial advice and computer and other services, as well as loans, to small and medium-sized companies. Generally its loans are less than £50,000 for ten to twenty years. In 1974 these two institutions were grouped under a single holding company known as Finance for Industry Limited (FFI). The initial share capital was held by the London and Scottish clearing banks and the Bank of England. When FFI expanded in November 1974 to enable £1,000 million over two years to be made available for medium-term loans for productive investment, other financial institutions agreed to subscribe to periodic issues of interest-bearing stock.

The London and provincial Stock Exchange trading floors in the United Kingdom and the Irish Republic are now grouped into a single dealing system for quoted securities, both public sector and private. Business is introduced by brokers who work on commission for buyers and sellers. Brokers must deal through jobbers, who make a market in stocks, which they deal in on their own account. New capital for industry and commerce can be raised through the Stock Exchange by share issues. Nearly all securities issued on the British market are in registered form. United Kingdom residents who hold bearer securities are required to deposit them with an authorised depository — a stockbroker, a bank or some other professional intermediary.

The government also directly competes, through its various national savings facilities, in the small savers' market. Facilities include the National Savings Certificate and the British Savings Bond (both maturity type securities); Save As You Earn (a contractual savings scheme); the Premium Savings Bond (accumulated interest is distributed by way of prizes determined by lot); and facilities offering small savers easy access to government stocks. The National and Trustee Savings Banks are deposit institutions which offer interest-bearing, on-call and long-term accounts. The Trustee Savings Banks, which also run cheque accounts, are expected to expand their range of services in due course. Many of the national savings facilities attract tax reliefs.

Sources of funds for investment
Table 5.2 shows the proportions in which non-financial companies derive capital funds from different sources. About half is generated internally, but much of the balance comes from bank borrowing.

Table 5.2. *Sources of capital funds of industrial and commercial companies, 1970-4*

	1970	1971	1972	1973	1974
	(percentages)				
Undistributed income	52	56	49	49	54
Investment grants	7	8	3	2	1
Other capital transfers	1	1	1	1	1
Bank borrowing	18	11	30	31	29
Other loans and mortgages	5	4	2	5	1
UK capital issues	3	5	6	1	—
Overseas	15	15	9	11	14
Total	100	100	100	100	100
	(£ millions)				
Total value	6,336	6,770	9,444	14,748	15,207

SOURCE: CSO, *Financial Statistics,* May 1975.

In 1973 about half each came from the secondary and deposit banks, but in 1969 nearly three-quarters had come from the deposit banks. The category 'other loans and mortgages' includes funds received from the special investment agencies and from insurance companies and pension funds.

2. Monetary Policy

Monetary policy aims both to assist fiscal policy in the management of overall demand in the economy and to prevent excessive loss of reserves through international movements of capital, particularly short-term funds. In pursuit of the latter the Bank of England deals in the foreign exchange market and imposes exchange control regulations; there are also other policies, particularly as regards interest rates, which often have the international situation in mind. When the pound is at a fixed exchange rate the Bank intervenes in the foreign exchange market to prevent movements outside the limits, but when, as at present, it is floating, interventions are confined to ensuring, so far as possible, that speculation does not push the exchange rate to unrealistic levels.

Domestic monetary policy is determined by the Treasury in consultation with the Bank of England and administered by the Bank. It aims to control demand through regulating the amount of outstanding credit and, to a lesser extent, through ensuring that the growth of the money supply is not excessive. There has been no arithmetic target for the growth of the money supply on either of its definitions, but policy has to some extent been influenced by the idea that the money supply should accommodate the real rate of growth of the economy plus the 'acceptable' rate of inflation, which would, of course, often be the current rate. As subsidiary objectives, policy seeks to minimize the cost of the interest burden on the national debt and to ensure the health and solvency of the major financial institutions.

In general, monetary policy has been much less important than fiscal policy in demand management in postwar Britain. This was for a number of reasons. The policy makers considered that — with some exceptions — the effect of the use of monetary policy was vague and hard to ascertain, with considerable uncertainty about the sectors of expenditure which would be affected. (Hire purchase controls were an exception to this.) Further, the authorities were constrained in their use of the interest rate weapon both by a desire to keep an orderly market in government securities and by the need to use interest rates primarily to encourage short-term capital inflows, or discourage short-term capital outflows, in the interests of the balance of payments.

Consequently, during most of the postwar period the main monetary weapons used by the authorities were two: first, the influencing of hire purchase transactions by altering the size of the deposits required and the length of time over which repayment had to be made; secondly, the setting of a physical limit to the advances made by the clearing banks, together with directions about the priorities which the banks should use. It was these restrictions on the lending behaviour of the clearing banks which led to the rise of the secondary banking sector (Table 5.1). From the time of the Radcliffe Committee's Report on monetary policy at the end of the 1950s, up to the beginning of the 1970s, there was very little evolution in the actual practice of monetary policy. Then in September 1971 a new system came into effect,[1] by which an attempt was made to replace the direct control on bank advances by a system of indirect control, described below; the Bank of England also ceased to intervene to maintain a steady rate of interest on medium- and long-term government stock.

---

[1] 'Competition and credit control', *Bank of England Quarterly Bulletin*, June 1971.

Debt management

The Bank of England deals in the market for government bonds (the gilt-edged market) in its capacity as banker and issuing house to the government. The government tends to receive a large proportion of its tax income in the first quarter, although public expenditure continues throughout the year; it also has long-term investment programmes which cannot be financed out of current income. It therefore needs to borrow both short- and long-term. In addition, a substantial amount of marketable government debt is outstanding (some £44,500 million in March 1975); some of this matures each year and requires refinancing. For these reasons the government broker, acting on behalf of the Bank, has to maximize his long-run sales of bonds to firm buyers.

In the past the authorities were prepared to buy all stock offered to them at the current price in order to secure an orderly market. It was felt that this led to excessive marketability of the banks' holdings, thus leaving little control over the money supply, and since 1971 the practice has been confined to stock with one year of less to maturity. All other stock is now bought solely at the authorities' discretion and at prices of their own choosing. The 'tap' stocks (current issues of different maturities) are no longer sold at a quoted price, but the government broker will accept bids for them. This has led to greater variability in the price of gilt-edged stocks as a whole and a decline in long-term holdings. The authorities now have greater scope for using the bond market as an instrument of monetary policy, but are faced with a bigger refinancing problem.

The Treasury bill market

Every week there is an issue of three-month Treasury bills, the size of which is determined by short-term financing and general policy needs. They are bought largely by the banks themselves, and on their behalf by the discount houses, as they are an important component of the banks' minimum reserve ratios. The Bank of England can exercise influence over a range of interest rates by varying the size and thus the price of the Treasury bill issue. If the discount houses are unable to cover the issue, they have the right to borrow cash from the Bank of England, usually for one week at the minimum lending rate, although this can vary. As this is a penal rate, in order to maintain their margins the discount houses must increase the rates they charge the banks.

The rates of interest in the Treasury bill market are less important than they used to be since the growth of the 'parallel' money markets, but if the Treasury bill issue is particularly small the banks are often forced to bid for money in the inter-bank or sterling certificate of deposit markets to make up their reserve ratios.

The minimum lending rate

As a general rule, the minimum lending rate, which replaced Bank rate in October 1972, is ½ per cent above Treasury bill rate rounded up to the nearest ¼ per cent. Unlike Bank rate, to which many other rates were tied, the minimum lending rate is only relevant to loans to the discount houses. In exceptional circumstances the Chancellor of the Exchequer can determine the rate independently and in November 1973 it was raised from 11¼ per cent to 13 per cent during the oil crisis. Such a use has purely psychological impact and gives an indication of the feelings of the authorities.

Regulation of financial institutions

The new regulations for financial institutions were drawn up after consultations in 1971 and reflect the changes which had taken place during the 1960s, particularly the growth of the secondary banks. The aim is to allow the authorities some control over the activities of the institutions without unduly interfering with competition between them or discriminating between different types of institution.

Technically the regulations and directives imposed by the Bank of England have no legal force and are observed voluntarily, but powers exist under the Bank of England Act 1946 to give them the force of law if necessary. The regulations fall into two groups: permanent day-to-day rules and those which the Bank invokes from time to time as circumstances warrant.

The permanent regulations require that all banks hold 12½ per cent of certain liabilities (chiefly sterling deposits of less than two years maturity, net foreign currency liabilities, net inter-bank sterling deposits and net sterling certificates of deposit) in certain specified assets. These are largely 'traditional' money market assets: balances at the Bank of England, Treasury bills, money at call with the London discount market, government stocks with a maturity of one year or less, local authority and commercial bills eligible for rediscount at the Bank of England and company tax reserve certificates. The banks themselves can determine what proportion of each asset they hold, with the exception of commercial bills which must not contribute more than 2 per cent and the deposit banks' holdings of cash at the Bank of England which must contribute a minimum of 1½ per cent. The supply of these assets is largely under the control of the authorities, so that they can make it easier or more difficult for the banks to make up their minimum reserve ratios. However, eligible liabilities include *net* inter-bank deposits and issues of sterling certificates of deposit which means that a bank can reduce its liabilities and thus increase its reserve ratio by lending to other banks and bidding for sterling certificates of deposit. There are special arrangements for the Northern Ireland banks in view of their particular relations with the Republic of Ireland and the financial needs arising out of the present emergency.

Finance houses must hold 10 per cent of their eligible liabilities (all deposits for less than two years other than those from banks) in the same assets.

The arrangements for discount houses were changed in July 1973, so that their total assets excluding certain ones from the public sector (largely of less than five years to maturity) must not exceed twenty times their capital and reserves. Although there is no longer any formal requirement to hold public sector debt, the Bank of England will only act as lender of last resort against approved securities, particularly Treasury bills.

Among the discretionary regulations, the Bank of England may, from time to time, call for special deposits. These are levied on all banks as a uniform percentage of eligible liabilities and must be deposited in cash at the Bank of England. Interest is payable at Treasury bill rate. They have the effect of increasing the minimum reserve ratio, as the banks have to sell liquid assets in order to pay the deposits and these must then be replaced. In addition a different rate of special deposits can be levied on the increase in overseas liabilities after a given date, or on the outstanding total of such liabilities.

In December 1973 an additional variation was introduced which allows the Bank of England to call for up to 50 per cent of the increase in interest-bearing eligible liabilities after a given date and above a specified rate of increase to be paid into non-interest-bearing special deposits. Subsequent comparisons are based on a three-month moving average. When this instrument has been used the penalties have varied from 5 to 50 per cent depending on the rate of excess growth. The scheme is designed to restrain the increase in the money supply and lending without rises in short-term interest rates.

The other main discretionary weapons are the power to restrict the interest paid on deposit accounts in order to protect the building societies and savings banks in competition for small savings, and the power to issue guidelines on the direction although not the total of lending. (QUALITATIVE MEASURES)

Hire purchase controls

Controls over the terms on which hire purchase lending can be conducted are strictly speaking under the control of the Secretary of State for Prices and Consumer Protection, not the monetary authorities, but they are generally regarded as a monetary instrument. The regulations lay down the minimum deposit and the maximum repayment period for different classes of consumer goods. Unlike other instruments their effect on demand is immediate, but they are discriminatory both between persons (hitting only those who cannot afford to pay cash) and between industries. Largely for these reasons their abolition was recommended by the Committee on Consumer Credit in 1971 and, with the lifting of restrictions in July of that year, it was widely believed that this recommendation had been followed. However, the authorities were reluctant to lose such a useful weapon and new restrictions were imposed in 1973.

*   *   *   *   *

The competition and credit control arrangements introduced in 1971, which replaced a system of ceilings on bank lending, aimed to influence the aggregate supply and allocation of credit through its cost, while also providing scope for the authorities to influence the direction of bank lending through directional guidance. The introduction in December 1973 of the supplementary deposits scheme has meant that the authorities once again have a more direct means of influencing the growth of money and credit than was provided for in the 1971 arrangements.

Chapter Six

EXTERNAL TRADE AND PAYMENTS

1. General Structure of the Balance of Payments

The United Kingdom has had a deficit on visible trade in all but a few years since the beginning of the nineteenth century. Usually the deficit has been more than matched by a surplus on invisible transactions, but between the First and Second World Wars this was tending to dwindle, while at the same time exports were declining in both value and volume, although imports were rather more stable. Consequently the balance of payments on current account is believed to have been in slight deficit in the years immediately preceding the Second World War.

In the postwar period the deficit on visible trade has on the whole increased (Table 6.1); it reached a peak of £5,264 million in 1974, and averaged some £3,600 million for the four years 1973-6. This,

Table 6.1. *United Kingdom balance of payments, 1920-76*

£ millions

	Visible trade (net)	Invisibles (net)	Current balance	Capital flows (net)	Balancing item	Official financing
1920	−148	+463	+315	−135	−132	−48
1925	−265	+296	+31	−78	+45	+2
1930	−283	+298	+15	−72	+64	−7
1938	−285	+220	−65	−182	−21	+268
1955	−313	+158	−155	−195	+121	+229
1960	−401	+156	−245	+286	+252	−293
1965	−223	+197	−26	−326	−1	+353
1970	−25	+758	+733	+573	+114	−1,420
1976	−3,592	+2,169	−1,423	−147	−267	+1,837

SOURCES: CSO, *United Kingdom Balance of Payments, 1965-1975,* London, HMSO, 1976; *Economic Trends,* March 1977; *Bank of England Quarterly Bulletin,* March 1974.

however, reflects the rise in turnover. In 1975 the value of imports was some twenty-six times as high as in 1938, whereas the value of exports was more than thirty times as high. In real terms the comparison is even more favourable, imports having risen less than threefold and exports nearly fourfold. For manufactures, on the other hand, the story is rather different, partly no doubt because of the dominating position of United Kingdom products at the beginning of the period. Between 1937 and 1975 imports of manufactures increased in volume five to six times and exports increased four times.

From 1925 until 1935 the United Kingdom's terms of trade improved, reaching a level that was only gradually regained through the 1950s and 1960s after a sharp deterioration in the late 1940s and early 1950s. The interwar improvement partly compensated for the worsening in the balance of trade in real terms, while the early postwar deterioration reduced the effect of the relative increase in the volume of exports. In 1973, however, because of the rise in commodity prices, the terms of trade moved violently against the United Kingdom and they have since stabilized at a level not much more favourable than that prevailing at the time of the Korean War.

The problem of a visible deficit has not in the past been as serious for the United Kingdom as for other developed countries, although if present trends continue it will become increasingly important. The United Kingdom was able to tolerate rapid growth in the volume of imports in the 1930s and 1950s partly because of favourable terms of trade. But broadly from the beginning of at least the 1960s, and probably in the 1970s until circumstances made it obviously impossible, the intention has been that a surplus on invisible account should finance a small trade deficit, an outflow of capital (first principally as investment, recently as aid) and any desired increase in the reserves. As the United Kingdom's widespread, though contracting, overseas commitments imply a substantial deficit on government account, this postulates an even bigger surplus on private services. The invisible balance has always in fact been positive, but since the middle of 1972 and particularly after the oil price increases the surplus on invisibles has been too small to offset the increased deficit on visible trade, so that the capital account, previously in surplus only in 1960-1 and 1970-1, has also financed part of the latter. The net flow of capital for private investment had previously been inward only in occasional years, but substantial net inflows were recorded in 1971, and from

1974 to 1976; the public sector capital account had its first large net inflow in 1973; this has remained a major source of finance. Apart from these long-term capital inflows, which will probably continue for some years at least, the other main source of finance until 1974 (as in the late 1940s) was the building up of sterling reserves by other countries.

Availability of North Sea oil from 1975 onwards should bring the net cost of oil imports down to below the 1973 level by 1980 (both by reducing imports and by providing export income from which continuing imports can be financed). By the mid-1980s net exports of oil could reverse the traditional deficit on visible trade. The surplus on property income may be greatly reduced by the interest and profits accruing to foreign participants in the exploitation of the oil, including those who have financed related imports of equipment. North Sea oil production is unlikely to necessitate a further increase in such imports or the diversion of output from export markets, and the surplus on non-oil trade that was usual before 1973 was restored in 1976. Net exports of oil, if they materialize, should thus make it possible to achieve the postwar goal of current surplus (although in the 1980s this will be needed to reduce external liabilities created by the post-1972 deficits).

2. The Commonwealth Preference and Sterling Area Systems

Perhaps the outstanding feature of British commercial policy over the past fifty years has been the establishment and subsequent dissolution of preferential arrangements of various kinds in favour of the Commonwealth and Sterling Area.

Though membership of the two areas overlapped to an important extent, there were in fact two systems, differing both in coverage and in organization. The Commonwealth Preference Area comprised all members of the Commonwealth, South Africa and the Irish Republic; the Sterling Area excluded one major Commonwealth country — Canada — and included a number of other countries, varying from time to time, within the British sphere of influence either politically or commercially.

The Commonwealth Preference Area originated in the 1930s with the extension of the previously limited duties on United Kingdom imports. This provided the opportunity for an area with special privileges to be formed, although the basic privilege was only exemption from the new restrictions.

The introduction of exchange controls and dollar pooling for the Sterling Area during the Second World War marked the beginning of a formally defined area. For its overseas members the change was from keeping reserves in London from habit and for convenience to being expected not only to keep them there but to accept co-ordination of their use according to the needs of the area as a whole. Freedom of action was particularly limited for some of the colonial countries, where the domestic currency issue still required complete sterling backing, and the only complete exception to the general rule was the Union of South Africa, which continued to keep a high proportion of its reserves in gold. The pooling and restrictions represented a reversal of the trend of the 1930s towards a reduction in effective United Kingdom direction of the monetary policies of the Sterling Area countries, particularly the independent ones.

In the early years after the Second World War the existence of exchange controls on payments to and from non-Sterling Areas gave the Sterling Area a further stimulus because of its exemption from the United Kingdom's controls. The United Kingdom also gave uniform and preferential quota treatment to Sterling Area products, and it gave uniform tariff treatment to goods originating in the Commonwealth Preference Area.[1] This uniformity was not reciprocated, however. Many Commonwealth countries gave British goods no tariff preferences or very few; some Sterling Area countries operated a generalized system of quotas and exchange controls that gave no preference to imports from other Sterling Area countries.

In the 1930s the United Kingdom had provided other Sterling Area countries, particularly the food producers, with a stable market; the central control of imports in the 1940s permitted long-term contracts that had a similar effect. In the 1950s and especially in the 1960s, however, the shift in the commodity composition of world trade made the existence of an organization providing complementary markets less important, and over the last fifteen or twenty years there has been a drastic re-orientation of preferential

---

[1] In one special case, sugar, the United Kingdom paid negotiated prices on fixed quantities of imports from the Commonwealth under the Commonwealth Sugar Agreement, the negotiated prices normally being well above world market prices. In the immediate postwar years it had operated a number of other commodity long-term bulk-purchasing agreements, but these had effectively disappeared by the early 1960s.

trading arrangements: the system of Commonwealth Preference and the Sterling Area was first eroded and then, in the process of negotiating entry to the European Communities, deliberately dismantled.

The restraints of the early postwar years which had been directed at discouraging expenditure outside the Sterling Area, and particularly in Dollar Area countries, lapsed for the independent Sterling Area countries as early as the 1950s. Such preferences as Overseas Sterling Area countries had given to Britain and to one another by means of exchange controls and quotas virtually disappeared, as did the similar preferences accorded by the United Kingdom.

The Sterling Area remained in being after 1960 because exchange controls were not applied to investment by United Kingdom residents in the Overseas Sterling Area—a privilege abolished when the pound was floated in 1972—but when sterling was devalued in November 1967 a number of Overseas Sterling Area countries did not change the par value of their own currencies correspondingly. These countries nevertheless continued to keep a large proportion of their foreign exchange reserves in British government assets. From 1968 onwards the United Kingdom guaranteed the greater part of these sterling reserves against devaluation by a series of agreements, in which Sterling Area countries undertook in return that the proportion of their reserves (though not the amount) held in sterling would be maintained at or above a prescribed figure. These arrangements were, however, allowed to lapse in 1974.

Meanwhile preferential margins in the United Kingdom tariff, which in 1961 was equivalent to about 7 per cent *ad valorem,* were being eroded in a number of ways. First, where duties were specific rather than *ad valorem,* rising prices steadily reduced the percentage preference margin. Secondly, where 'most favoured nation' duties on products paying no duty if imported from the Commonwealth into the United Kingdom—in practice most manufactured products—were reduced in the course of the GATT negotiations, the margin of preference was automatically reduced. Thirdly, the creation of the European Free Trade Association (EFTA) during the years 1959-67 diluted the effect of United Kingdom preferences to the Commonwealth by putting Commonwealth and EFTA manufactures on the same tariff footing. There is some evidence that this led to trade diversion in favour of EFTA. Finally, unilateral tariff changes led to the reduction or dilution of preferences, initially affecting only United Kingdom exports to the Commonwealth. However, at the beginning of 1972 the United

Kingdom took two major steps: it introduced a preferential duty on Commonwealth cotton textiles and clothing, formerly duty-free, and a system of generalized preferences for manufactures other than textiles from developing countries, putting them on a par with the developing countries in the Commonwealth.

Thus, even had Britain not sought to join the EEC, the Commonwealth Preference and Sterling Area systems were rapidly declining in importance during the 1950s and 1960s; but this decision amounted to a death blow. The psychological impact of the abortive negotiations of 1957-8 was itself important, while the creation of EFTA, the free trade association of Britain, the Scandinavian countries, Portugal, Switzerland and Austria, had a direct effect on trade between the United Kingdom and the Commonwealth. In the 1961-3 negotiations for entry into the EEC the United Kingdom was still seeking to retain some part of the Commonwealth Preference system, but by the time of the final negotiations for entry this special treatment had been reduced to medium-term guarantees on United Kingdom imports of Commonwealth sugar and New Zealand butter and cheese, association with the Community for some minor Commonwealth countries and territories,[1] and easier Community tariff treatment for a handful of products of interest to Commonwealth producers.

At present, then, United Kingdom commercial policy is in the final stages of transition from the old Commonwealth Preference and Sterling Area systems to the new Community system. If all goes according to the Treaty of Accession, tariffs between Britain and the rest of the enlarged Community will have been abolished by July 1977 and the Common External Tariff will have been fully adopted by the United Kingdom along with the CAP. Britain will also, of course, participate in any developments of the common commercial policy of the EEC.

3. Trade Liberalization

The other major development of the postwar period in the sphere of trade policy has been the liberalization of trade on a multilateral basis, in common with all other members of the EEC, through

---

[1] The major African Commonwealth countries already have association agreements with the Six, while Asian and developed Commonwealth countries are being treated like the rest of the world. In 1975 the EEC introduced preferential tariffs and increased quotas for some imports from developing countries.

tariff reductions, and through the abolition of quantitative import restrictions and exchange controls.

As a founder-member of the IMF and the Organization for European Economic Cooperation (OEEC), Britain directed its commercial policies during the 1950s towards restoring the convertibility of sterling (associated with the removal of exchange controls on current though not on capital transactions) and towards the abolition of quota restrictions on imports. Formal convertibility under article 8 of the IMF was adopted in 1961, but the pound had in effect been convertible for non-residents since February 1955, when the Exchange Equalization Account began to support the rate for non-convertible sterling, previously sold for foreign exchange only at a discount.

Meanwhile, quota restrictions on Sterling Area imports, which had been of little significance since 1955, were effectively abolished in 1958. The removal of quotas on imports from the OEEC and the Dollar Area took slightly longer, until mid-1960 and 1961 respectively. Quotas on Japanese goods and imports from the Sino-Soviet bloc were maintained into the 1960s, but there was steady progress towards liberalization. In contrast, a system of quotas on imports of cotton textiles and clothing from developing countries was gradually built up over the same years. However, apart from this, some restrictions on imports from Sino-Soviet countries and a few quotas remaining on minor items, physical controls on United Kingdom imports had disappeared by the end of the 1960s.

Thus the sole major instrument of commercial policy, save in respect of farm produce, was then as it is now the tariff. Britain's 'most favoured nation' tariff has always had negligible or zero duties on raw materials, but used to give considerable protection to manufactures. Tariff reductions from the early postwar tariff-cutting programme under GATT, which culminated in the Geneva Round of 1956, made little difference to this situation. As elsewhere, significant tariff reductions began with the Dillon Round and were carried on in the Kennedy Round on a greatly increased scale. Between 1960 and 1972 the United Kingdom's 'most favoured nation' tariff on manufactures was reduced by roughly two-fifths, with reductions of a half applying to a high proportion of finished goods, especially machinery and vehicles. At the beginning of 1972 the average United Kingdom tariff on non-agricultural goods was only a few percentage points higher than the Common External Tariff of the EEC, where formerly it had been considerably higher.

4. Exchange Rate Policy

Before the First World War there had been little change in exchange rates, and it was assumed that this situation would continue after the war; the fact that the value of the pound in terms of the dollar had fallen sharply during and immediately after the war was considered a result of temporary strain because of high imports and restricted exports. (Only the dollar rate was considered in devaluation decisions and this remained generally true until the early 1970s.) The decision to return to the prewar rate ($4.86) was thus treated as a timing decision rather than a decision about the appropriate rate. The rise in the rate in early 1925 was both a confirmation of this assumption and an indication that the timing could be brought forward. That adjustments to domestic prices might be needed was recognized, but this was treated as a necessary cost, not as a possible influence on the decision. The appreciation, followed by the failure of United States prices to rise as rapidly as expected and France's return to gold with a devaluation, made British exports uncompetitive in those markets in the late 1920s. The adjustments necessary to hold the new exchange rate proved to be impossible and, combined with the loss of confidence in other currencies, to threaten a flight of capital from sterling in 1931. The gold standard was accordingly abandoned for the rest of the 1930s.

The government did not intervene to slow the resulting fall in the value of the pound. But in 1932 when it began to recover (at about $3.50), control was introduced, directed at preventing disturbances in external markets from hurting domestic policy. (It was in this year too that import duties were generally introduced and the Sterling Area began to be encouraged.) The Exchange Equalization Account provided, through dealings in Treasury bills, some insulation from short-term capital flows. The value of the pound in terms of other currencies rose through the 1930s, rising above the former rate at the end of the period and losing its competitive position.

After the war a lower parity was held at $4.03, helped by exchange controls. An attempt to restore convertibility in 1947 under the terms of the 1945 Anglo-American loan agreement failed, and in September 1949 the rate was lowered to $2.80. For the United Kingdom this change was perhaps a reaction more to capital account problems than to import increases; controls still kept these to a low level. As the devaluation immediately preceded a large rise in commodity prices, it increased their effect. For the

United Kingdom its size was, however, reduced by the number of countries inside and outside the Sterling Area that maintained their currencies' existing parities with the pound. The principal effect was thus to reinforce the planned diversion of imports from and exports to the Dollar Area by the Sterling Area as a whole.

Throughout the 1950s and the first half of the 1960s maintaining the parity unchanged was a central consideration in the United Kingdom's external policy. The ability to maintain the rate was helped by the introduction of swap arrangements among central banks. The possibility of devaluation to improve the current balance was discussed from the early 1960s, but, as in the 1920s, attempts were made to adjust the economy to the exchange rate, until huge short-term outflows made inevitable the movement to a lower rate ($2.40) in November 1967. The subsequent improvement in the current balance was slow to materialize and was partly the result of growing world trade, but it was widely accepted as a demonstration of the success of the devaluation, and opposition to a more flexible exchange rate was correspondingly weakened. In 1971 the floating and devaluation of the dollar caused the pound to float for four months and, although the mistake of returning to an overvalued parity was made yet again, in the summer of 1972 floating and devaluation were no longer feared and unfamiliar, and could be introduced without delay. Since then, the pound has fallen rather more rapidly than can be explained simply by changes in price competitiveness. The fall has occurred in discrete changes between temporary plateaux rather than continuously.

Movements in the exchange rate have of course affected the invisible balance and the capital account as well as visible trade. Property income, in particular, has risen through devaluation, as sterling-denominated payments abroad do not change, while foreign currency receipts increase in sterling terms. Such benefits will be reduced as payments denominated in foreign currency on loans from abroad become more important, but these would have to rise more than is probable before the situation would be completely reversed. Similarly, on capital account, the borrowing in non-sterling currency is a potential burden. But until the offering of exchange rate guarantees, which have now been withdrawn, devaluation, by increasing the sterling value of reserves of foreign currency, improved the ratio between these and short-term sterling liabilities.

5. Imports and Exports

The volume of imports of goods was about four times as great in 1976 as at the turn of the century (Table 6.2); it doubled in the first sixty years and has doubled again in the last fifteen years. Two world wars, the great depression, and restrictions and import duties of varying severity hampered import development during the former period. On the other hand, from the early 1960s an unprecedented import growth accompanied the import liberalization measures already described and a rapid rise in home demand. In general, import growth lagged behind the increase in national product in volume terms during the first half of this century, but far outstripped it in later years, with imports of manufactures rising particularly fast. Until the beginning of the 1970s fuel imports also increased very rapidly, whereas imports of food, beverages and tobacco and of basic materials have throughout risen relatively slowly.

In value terms the ratio of imports to national product has changed little in the last twenty-five years, import prices having risen much more slowly than domestic prices until 1973. There have, however, been big changes in the composition of imports. Imports of food, beverages and tobacco shrank from almost half of the total value in 1935-8 to about a sixth in 1975-6 and imports of basic materials accounted for only 10 per cent of all merchandise imports in 1976, compared with 26 per cent before the Second World War and about 30 per cent in the early 1950s (Table 6.3). On the other hand, fuel imports had, by the 1950s, grown from practically nothing at the turn of the century into a group which regularly constituted about 10-12 per cent of the total until 1974, when this share rose to about 20 per cent as a result of the increase in oil prices. At the same time the share of the total accounted for by imports of manufactures rose in the 1970s to over 50 per cent, although up to the mid-1950s it had been only about 20 per cent, as in 1935-8.

The volume of food imports rose by about 50 per cent between 1900 and 1937, but then remained below the 1937 level until the late 1950s. This was partly due to the incentives given to British agriculture during and after the war. But imports of food per head of the population during the last twelve years have been on the whole lower than in 1960-3. Imports of basic materials were about the same in 1975-6 as in 1938, but imports per unit of manufacturing output were lower by nearly three-fifths.

Table 6.2. *Imports of goods, 1900-76*

Volume indices, $1961 = 100^a$

(A) Manufactures

	Finished manufactures			Chemicals	Textiles	Total
	Machinery	Transport equipment	Total			
1938	40	28	43	41	31	54
1950	29	23	25	44	65	43
1955	46	54	41	60	57	67
1957	56	75	51	64	66	66
1952-5	44	64	37	50	46	53
1956-9	59	78	56	68	66	68
1960-3	98	133	105	109	98	104
1964-7	166	194	166	173	113	147
1968-71	259	480	264	276	149	212
1972-3	439	848	466	395	215	314
1974	528	810	532	464	241	361
1976	524[b]	1,017	551[b]	460	263	365[b]

(B) All goods

	Manufactures	Food beverages, tobacco	Basic materials	Fuels	Total goods
1900					51
1913					68
1929					77
1938	54	98	96	29	76
1950	43	78	94	41	65
1955	67	89	102	75	82
1957	66	93	103	70	83
1952-5	53	83	96	62	74
1956-9	68	95	98	76	84
1960-3	104	102	101	107	103
1964-7	147	103	105	147	123
1968-71	212	104	108	197	152
1972-3	314	105	109	224	192
1974	361	102	104	215	207[c]
1976	365[b]	104	103	176	206[c]

SOURCES: Department of Trade and Industry; London and Cambridge Economic Service, *Key Statistics of the British Economy 1900-1970,* London, Times, 1971; NIESR estimates.

[a]Indices based on 1954, 1961 and 1970 linked through over-lapping years 1952-5 and 1964-7.

[b]Includes part of 'continental shelf transactions'.

[c]Includes gold coins; this inclusion is estimated to have added about 0.5 per cent to the volume index in 1974-5 and it would probably be less in previous years.

Falls in the ratio of imports of materials to industrial production were especially sharp during the two world wars, although apparently continuing on a much smaller scale in peacetime also.[1] The chief reasons have been the decline of the textile and other industries which are heavily dependent on imported materials, the partial replacement by synthetic products of natural fibres and rubber, and the new applications of manufactured materials as substitutes for natural ones, for example the use of steel instead of timber in building.

During the first half of the century the development of the internal combustion engine for mass transport and industrial use was accompanied by a spectacular rise in the volume of fuel imports. Not surprisingly there has been a marked slowing down more recently. During the twenty years up to 1973 the annual rate of increase still averaged about 7 per cent, but after the huge rises in oil prices in late 1973 the volume of fuel imports fell by nearly a fifth in two years, and then North Sea oil production started.

The volume of imports of manufactures regained its prewar level in five years after the First World War, but the same process took ten years after the Second World War. Subsequently, however, there has been a spectacular rise in most groups of manufactures. This applied most notably to finished goods, where the rise has often been 20-30 per cent or more in one year. Between 1956-9 and 1974-6 total imports of finished manufactures increased over ninefold in volume and, within this group, transport equipment grew elevenfold. In value terms the share of machinery and transport equipment was over three times as large a proportion of total imports in 1976 as it had been in the late 1950s, whereas over the same period chemical and textiles nearly doubled their shares.

---

[1]M.FG. Scott, *A Study of United Kingdom Imports,* Cambridge University Press, 1963, pp. 28-9. On a definition which includes non-ferrous metals, Scott estimates, however, that imports of materials increased by about 40 per cent from 1900 to 1938.

Table 6.3   *Changes in the composition of imports,[a] 1935-76*

Percentages

	1935 –8[b]	1948 –55	1956 –63	1964 –7	1968 –71	1972 –3	1974 –5	1976
Machinery[c]	3	2	5	8	11	13	13	13
Transport equipment[c]	1	1	2	3	5	7	6	7
Chemicals	2	3	4	5	6	6	6	7
Textiles and clothing	3	3	3	4	5	5	5	5
Other manufactures	12	11	14	20	23	25	23	22
Total manufactures	*21*	*20*	*28*	*40*	*50*	*56*	*53*	*54*
Food, beverages and tobacco	47	39	37	30	23	20	17	16
Basic materials	26	32	23	18	15	12	10	10
Fuels	5	9	12	11	11	11	19	19
Total non-manufactures	*78*	*80*	*72*	*59*	*49*	*43*	*46*	*45*
Total goods[d]	100	100	100	100	100	100	100	100

SOURCES: W. Beckerman and Associates, *The British Economy in 1975,* Cambridge University Press, 1965, p.149, Table 5.1; Department of Trade and Industry.

[a]Retained imports up to 1969, total imports 1970-5. In the years 1964-7 and 1968-71 the differences between retained and total imports were under 0.5 per cent for each main commodity group.

[b]1936-8 for machinery, transport equipment, textiles and clothing.

[c]SITC groups 711.4-6 are excluded from machinery and included in transport equipment. Certain equipment for continental shelf operations is included in 1975 and 1976 only.

[d]Including miscellaneous imports, other than gold coins, which are included in the official statistics for 1974-6.

In considering the recent growth in imports of manufactures it is important to remember that, whereas their volume is estimated to have increased about two and a half times from 1913 to 1959 for all industrial countries, there was little change in the corresponding figures for the United Kingdom. Over this period the import content of supplies of manufactured goods in the United Kingdom decreased from 17 per cent to 6 per cent and it is estimated that in 1959 imports of manufactures per head of population were about 10 per cent lower than in 1899 and a third lower than in 1913 and 1929. Consequently it seems reasonable to assume that British imports were abnormally low prior to the strong upsurge which produced a fivefold increase between 1957 and 1974-6 in imports of manufactures per head.[1]

Between 1900 and 1973 the United Kingdom's share of the world export trade in manufactures fell from 33 per cent to 9 per cent (a level which it has since maintained), although the importance of production for export in total United Kingdom output was roughly the same at both dates — about a quarter of GNP. Over the same period dramatic changes occurred in the composition of exports. Among commodities there was a sustained decline in the share of textiles in total exports of manufactures, and a corresponding increase in sales of chemical products, machinery and transport equipment. Among foreign markets there was a fluctuating balance between Sterling Area and West European customers, the former becoming dominant in the interwar years and the latter gaining in relative importance in the 1960s (Table 6.4).

The spread of industrialization abroad — through Germany and North America in the late nineteenth century, and through the rest of Europe, Russia, Japan and major Commonwealth territories in the twentieth — was the key factor determining these trends in export levels and structure. The reduction in Britain's share of output of manufactures that this implied in itself contributed to the reduction in her share of world trade. But more important was a continuous failure to adapt to the new patterns of competition and comparative advantage thrown up by the general economic growth.

This deterioration took place in two phases, separated in time by the Second World War. The first was characterized by a loss of cost advantages in traditional exports. The early specialization in labour-intensive lines such as coal and cotton became increasingly inappropriate in the 1920s as textile industries developed in Asia and mining expanded in the Netherlands and central Europe. Losses in cost competitiveness in iron and steel production *vis-à-vis* Germany and the United States were another important factor. In part, this reflected genuine productivity differences — the British capital stock was older and the labour force slow to adjust to the new industrial order — but the over-valuation of sterling after the gold standard was readopted in 1925 also contributed to the disparities between the United Kingdom's export prices and those of its competitors. The United Kingdom thus failed to profit from growth in advanced economies and by the 1930s the bulk of its

---

[1]Estimates in this paragraph are from A. Maizels, *Industrial Growth and World Trade,* Cambridge University Press, 1963.

export trade was concentrated on the preferential Sterling Area markets. The adverse terms of trade, and hence lower real incomes, encountered by the primary producing countries in the 1930s thus meant declining markets for British goods. The United Kingdom

Table 6.4. *Changes in the area and commodity structures of exports, 1900-76*

	1900 −10	1920 −30	1931 −8	1948 −55	1956 −60	1961 −5	1966 −70	1971 −6
	(percentages)							
Western Europe	33	30	28	26	28	36	39	50
Sterling Area outside Europe	31	37	43	48	42	35	28	20
North America	11	11	10	11	15	14	17	14
Rest of world	25	22	19	15	15	15	16	16
Machinery and transport equipment	11	8	18	37	41	42	41	40
Chemicals	5	4	7	7	8	9	10	11
Textiles	38	33	25	15	8	6	5	4
Metals and metal manufactures	13	12	12	12	13	12	12	10
Other manufactures	15	24	17	15	16	18	16	18
Total manufactures	*82*	*81*	*79*	*86*	*86*	*87*	*84*	*83*
Non-manufactures	*18*	*19*	*21*	*14*	*14*	*13*	*16*	*17*
				(£ millions)				
Total value[a]	342	757	422	2,340	3,367	4,210	6,466	15,291

SOURCES: Department of Trade and Industry; London and Cambridge Economic Service, *Key Statistics of the British Economy 1900-70.*
[a]Annual average of years covered.

lost ground in a contracting volume of world trade and the potential direct contribution of exports to GNP growth was much reduced.

In the second, postwar, phase of British export growth, the basis for trade shifted emphatically away from the exchange of manufactures for primary products with the Commonwealth and towards an exchange of manufactured goods with other industrialized countries. There was some further erosion of export shares on the earlier pattern, one notable example being the substitution of Japanese iron and steel in Australian and New Zealand imports during the trade liberalization of the mid-1950s. However, the striking feature of that period was the elevation of exports of engineering products to a role no less dominant than that of textiles at the turn of the century, and this was a position to which the commodity mixes of other leading trading nations also converged. In this new environment, in which competitiveness was generated not so much by cost advantages as by aggressive marketing and willingness to meet ever-changing technical standards, the British share of the fast-expanding world trade in manufactures proved extremely vulnerable. It fell from 25 to 9.5 per cent between 1950 and 1975, and two-thirds of the overall decline in the share of world trade since 1900 thus occurred after 1950.

Attempts to explain this diminishing participation in world trade have revolved around two fundamental structural problems of British industry. First, the suppliers of exportable goods, while successfully maintaining their existing stock of machinery, have failed to invest in new techniques or to diversify into new fast-growing product lines. Secondly, the range of exported goods has become very similar to that entering domestic consumption, so that exports are no longer complementary to but rather are competitive with production for the home market. This has meant that British industries depending on scale economies for cost advantages in trade have suffered in comparison with their EEC or North American competitors because of the slow growth of the British economy as a whole. Moreover, in the pursuit of full employment, domestic demand has been regularly managed close to or beyond its productive potential; producers have had little capacity available to meet new export contracts, and little profit incentive given the combination of high domestic inflation and fixed exchange rates during the 1960s.

The devaluation of 1967 and the subsequent transition to a floating rate in 1972 removed this last constraint and exports of manufactures have clearly benefited (Table 6.5), growing in volume terms by $6\frac{1}{2}$ per cent per annum between 1967 and 1976 (2 per cent per annum less than world trade) as against 3 per cent per annum (5 per cent less than world trade) in the period 1960-7.

Table 6.5. *Exports of goods, 1900-76*

Volume indices, 1961 = 100[a]

| | Manufactures | | | | | | Non- manu- factures | Total goods |
	Machin- ery[b]	Chemi- cals	Textiles	Metals	Other	Total		
1900	9	12	341	35	28	45	n.a.	48
1913	21	23	445	66	50	70	n.a.	83
1929	28	27	303	68	60	65	n.a.	67
1937	23	26	220	53	50	51	n.a.	54
1950	73	45	173	83	90	82	70	82
1950-5	76	51	151	76	86	80	74	79
1956-60	92	78	117	97	88	92	89	92
1961-5	106	115	103	102	112	107	107	107
1966-70	133	168	112	119	159	136	130	135
1971-6	180	274	156	143	266	195	180	191

SOURCES: Maizels, *Industrial Growth and World Trade;* Department of Trade and Industry; NIESR estimates.

[a] Indices based on 1954, 1961 and 1970 linked through overlapping years 1950-5 and 1961-5.

[b] Includes transport equipment.

6. Invisibles

The invisible surplus has fallen in real value since the 1920s and prospects for parts of it are not favourable. Of the three components of the account, property income has always provided the major source of funds, services have occasionally been in deficit and only in recent years in surplus on the same scale as property income, while transfers have always been in deficit.

After the First World War, shipping receipts, the traditional source of invisible earnings, fell because freight rates and Britain's share of shipping were lower. But in spite of another large fall after the Second World War, in which the merchant fleet was reduced by a quarter, the balance remained positive until the 1950s, since when it has been in deficit. The United Kingdom share of tonnage has continued to fall and freight costs have grown faster on imports than on exports. Deficits are likely to continue because of rising oil costs and the increasing volume of shipping. The surplus on civil aviation has in the past usually been sufficient to balance the shipping deficit. On travel, although there was a deficit in the early years, there has been a rising surplus since 1974. Other private services, principally insurance and banking, have had a continuously increasing surplus. They suffered least after both wars and are less sensitive to conditions in the United Kingdom. However, they cannot alone provide a substantial surplus on services.

Net property income increased rapidly from 1960, when its money value was about the same as in the 1920s, to 1973. After the liquidation of British overseas investment to the amount of over £1,000 million in the Second World War, it is still much lower in real terms than it was in the interwar period. The surplus will now be reduced by the interest payments on public sector borrowing and by the returns on increased private overseas investment in the United Kingdom.

Private transfers have never been large. Government transfers and services are a new postwar deficit item, although it rose only slowly after 1962 and fell in the late 1960s. Expenditure on administrative services has increased rapidly during the postwar period, faster than the rate of inflation. Aid payments stagnated until 1971, and there was a slow growth in military spending at current prices. There has been a rise in net transfers since 1972 because of net contributions to the EEC, which will increase substantially in coming years.

7. Capital Balance

The reversal of the previous net outflow of capital for private investment is one of the major changes in the United Kingdom balance of payments in the last few years. It has been the result of a very slow growth of investment, particularly portfolio investment, from the United Kingdom (except that financed from loans raised abroad), combined with increasing overseas investment in the United Kingdom, particularly in securities and North Sea oil. The outflows, even in the 1950s, were small in real value compared with those of the 1920s and 1930s. The flows of capital in both directions, however, remain very large compared with those of other countries except the United States.

In contrast to the long-term position, short-term liabilities have normally exceeded assets. The growth of the Eurodollar market has meant a very rapid rise in recent years in both assets and liabilities

(Table 6.6), but the net inflow of short-term capital has increased partly because United Kingdom interest rates have been relatively high.

The preferred form of short-term capital inflows has been official deposits, particularly those of sterling countries, whose holdings have fluctuated least. These had always existed as both the working balances and the long-term holdings of Sterling Area and other countries, but during the Second World War they increased sharply and were more clearly distinguished from other British liabilities. At that time most of the sterling reserves were held by India, Pakistan and Ceylon, with smaller amounts held by the colonial territories, and holdings by Australia, New Zealand and South Africa comparable with those of North America and Europe. The official attitude to them seems to have changed from worry in the 1930s about their growing size in relation to United Kingdom reserves; anxiety to prevent their reduction and encourage their increase during the late 1940s when their withdrawal could have increased the deficit on the balance of payments; renewed concern over their size in the 1950s and 1960s when the need for finance was less pressing; to efforts to preserve and increase them again in the

Table 6.6. *External assets and liabilities, 1962 and 1975*

£ millions

	1962	1975
Assets		
Private investment abroad	8,070	23,400
Public sector lending etc.	710	2,165
Banking and commercial claims	2,265	66,000
Reserves	1,540	2,700
Total identified external assets	12,585	94,265
Liabilities		
Overseas investment in private sector	3,165	14,095
Overseas loans to government and investment in public sector	3,806	7,872
Banking and commercial liabilities	2,965	67,680
Other public sector capital	1,189	2,858
Total identified external liabilities	11,125	92,505

SOURCE: *Bank of England Quarterly Bulletin,* June 1975; June 1976.

1970s. A return to worry in 1976 led to an offer of medium-term foreign currency bonds as a substitute, but only a small proportion of holdings was converted. During the 1950s the Middle East became an important holder and the balances held by the colonial territories increased, while those of the Asian members of the Commonwealth were reduced. The total increased in the early 1970s because of the trade surpluses of the Overseas Sterling Area, particularly those of the oil-producing countries, but the whole increase was lost in 1975 and 1976.

Sterling balances provided a form of external support for the balance of payments throughout the period, particularly in the 1940s. The need for official assistance in the late 1960s followed the declining importance of this traditional source of finance. Finally, although some public borrowing occurred in the 1960s and it increased in 1971 and 1972, the major increase came in 1973 and 1974. All the traditional forms of government borrowing then rose (except sales of government stocks, perhaps because they are denominated in sterling), but they became much less important than the new method of using foreign banks. This expedient provided the relative freedom from policy constraints on the United Kingdom that the use of sterling balances offered until the 1950s. In 1975, however, these forms of public borrowing fell sharply, and there has since been a return to official (IMF) assistance.

In the 1930s, and again in the 1950s and 1960s, the official objective was not merely to balance payments but to increase reserves. They were considered too low because the large volume of capital movements and the short-term liabilities, such as the sterling balances, made necessary some protection against sudden withdrawals that might reduce the reserves to below a working balance. This fear has been reduced by floating currencies, but the level of the floating rate itself depends partly on confidence in the ability of the reserves to sustain a temporary outflow.

Reserves rose immediately after the First World War and more slowly in the late 1920s. They rose rapidly after 1932 to reach a level in 1938 that permitted a large outflow of short-term capital. After the Second World War, except for a peak about 1950, they rose slowly until the early 1960s, when fluctuations began, followed by a sharp fall until 1968. Gold was the major part of the reserves between the wars and as late as 1955 it accounted for 94 per cent; since then foreign exchange has become more important. In 1970 and 1971 gold holdings fell, while foreign exchange reserves increased rapidly. Part of this increase was lost in 1972 and there were further small falls in 1975 and 1976.

Controls on capital movements began as informal consultation, particularly on the timing of foreign issues, in the late 1920s. They may have thus prevented temporary difficulties, although they had little net effect. In the 1930s they increased, and they were replaced by full exchange control in the Second World War. After the war control continued, and the use of United Kingdom funds for overseas investment has been increasingly restricted to investments which promise immediate returns. The result has been an increase in investment financed from unremitted profits and foreign borrowing. Portfolio investment is limited by the use of a pool of investment currency, preventing any increase financed from the United Kingdom. The controls, which at first applied only to investment outside the Sterling Area, were extended to developed countries within the area 'voluntarily' in 1966 and completely in 1972. Inward investment has also been controlled to ensure that the major part is financed from abroad, not from local borrowing. The ending of the net outflow of private investment has thus been consistent with official policy since the war and particularly since the early 1960s.

Chapter Seven

THE MANAGEMENT OF THE BRITISH ECONOMY

1. Objectives

The purpose of managment is to alter the course of the economy in order to achieve certain objectives — that is, to improve its performance in some way. During the postwar period there has been some change in the emphasis laid on different policy objectives in Britain. First of all, the experience of the war had convinced politicians — and the electorate — that full employment could be attained; the proposition could not be defended that work could be found for all in time of war but not in time of peace. Already, before the end of the war, the coalition government had committed itself to full employment policies, and the Labour government elected in 1945 accepted the preservation of full employment as its dominant economic objective. Secondly, Britain had emerged from the war with a huge imbalance in its overseas trade; the second main objective was to right this imbalance by raising exports and holding down imports. In those early years not much was heard about economic growth, because the concept was probably rather inapposite in a period of reconstruction; the emphasis was simply on more and more production. The idea of an underlying growth-rate which could be accelerated by economic policy was as yet absent. Finally, in the early postwar years not many policy makers saw the problem of rising prices as a long-term chronic problem; it was more widely held to be a temporary problem of postwar shortages. In the years up to 1950 there was a much greater fear of a possible post-recovery depression than there was of inflation.

In the 1950s, which was a period of Conservative government, the full employment commitment was maintained. We find the balance of payments objective frequently stated in a rather different way: policy makers constantly referred to the need to maintain 'the strength of sterling' and to preserve Britain's role as a world banker. Gradually, as the decade wore on, there was a growing realization that the problem of rising prices was not just a temporary or cyclical problem, but a continuing one. The price objective was a much more ambitious one then than now, in that policy makers were concerned if a rise in prices in any year exceeded 3 per cent.

Towards the end of the 1950s a new concern arose, or at least an old concern was phrased in a different way. As international comparisons of growth-rates became available, it became clear that Britain was a slow-growth country. It gradually became an explicit objective of economic policy to accelerate the rate of economic growth. New instruments were devised and new institutions established to this end (they are discussed in the next section). However, in the mid-1960s this new objective of economic growth came into sharp conflict with the balance of payments objective. It was in fact the latter objective which dominated policy from 1964, not only up to the time of devaluation in 1967, but up to the beginning of 1969.

Finally, towards the end of the period, there were further changes in emphasis. From 1966 onwards governments of both persuasions accepted a higher level of unemployment than they would have done before. In Britain, as in other industrial countries, the price objective became less ambitious, as the difficulties of finding any effective means of moderating the price rise became more apparent. And, with the floating of the exchange rate in July 1972, the form of the balance of payments objective changed. Both before devaluation, and indeed after it, the government was concerned to maintain a certain fixed parity for sterling, and the balance of payments objective could be expressed as the defence of the exchange rate. As from July 1972 this ceased to be so; the objective of an adequate balance of payments was still there, of course, but the exchange rate became an instrument of policy rather than an objective in its own right.

The bulk of economic policy in this period was concerned with one or more of four economic objectives — full employment, economic growth, an adequate balance of payments and stable prices. However, this is not an exhaustive list; for example, governments also had regional policies and policies which aimed to redistribute income. The government inherited from the 1930s the concept of depressed areas — rechristened in the postwar period Development Areas. These were areas where unemployment tended to be higher than in the country as a whole, and a long succession of policies — for example, subsidizing employment in the Development Areas and forbidding the building of new factories in areas where the demand for labour was high — were designed to check the centripetal tendencies of British industry. For the redistribution of income or wealth, no government had precise, quantified objectives. Labour governments tended to stress in particular the inequalities in the distribution of wealth, and introduced legislation on both capital gains and capital transfers. Conservative governments tended to stress the need for adequate reward for talent, particularly managerial talent, and the changes which they made in income tax rates and allowances often had this objective in mind.

2. Institutions and Instruments

Institutions in Britain would appear to be well designed for a strong, coherent, centralized, economic policy. Central governments in Britain are not faced with a division of powers, as in the United States, nor with powerful federal states, as in Western Germany; nor do they have the problems of coalition governments, as in the Netherlands or Belgium. Consequently there is nothing in the party system to prevent the elaboration of a coherent economic policy, and the Parliamentary system normally allows governments to pass any legislation required without any great difficulty. There are not many constraints in the Parliamentary or legal fields to hinder policy makers. Further, the country has had, from early on, a comparatively advanced apparatus of economic statistics; its national accounts, for example, were developed early and are highly detailed, and the government throughout the postwar period has had reasonably high level economic advice from economists well trained in Keynesian modes of thinking. Throughout most of the period economic policy has been highly centralized in the Treasury, and it has generally been true that if the Chancellor of the Exchequer and the Prime Minister together decided on a course of economic policy they were usually able to carry it through. Parliament's contribution to economic policy was relatively small.

There are two qualifications to this general picture, of economic policy being essentially decided by the Prime Minister and the Chancellor of the Exchequer on the advice of the Treasury. At various times the Governor of the Bank of England has been accepted as a third partner, with an independent view. How far this has been true has depended both on the complexion of the government and on the personality of the Governor. Secondly, there was a short period of about three years, from 1964 to 1967, when a new department, which had been set up in 1964, had some significant influence — the Department of Economic Affairs. Indeed it had been set up by the incoming Labour government specifically to provide a countervailing force to that of the Treasury, and in the early years of the Labour government it did succeed to some extent in sponsoring ideas other than those of short-term demand management. However, it was essentially the department which was supposed to bring about the acceleration of economic growth; as it became clearer that the balance of payments difficulties of the country would prevent any such acceleration, its power waned, and it ceased to have any important influence on economic policy well before its actual demise in 1969.

Some generalizations are possible about the instruments of economic policy which have been preferred in Britain; here, too, there have been changes over time. In the early postwar years, the main instruments used were physical controls. Industry's basic raw materials were allocated and there was fairly extensive consumer rationing. Indeed Britain took longer than many other countries to dismantle the full apparatus of physical controls; for example, rationing of butter, cheese, margarine, cooking fats and meat continued until 1954, and of house coal until 1958. Steel allocation continued until 1953 and building licences did not end until 1954. So physical controls were still quite important instruments of policy up to the early 1950s.

Thereafter, more traditional instruments of economic policy took over the dominant role. In general, it is true to say that fiscal instruments have been preferred to monetary instruments — certainly if one restricts the comparison to the traditional monetary instruments of open market operations and interest rate changes. There is each year a major fiscal decision at the time of the regular annual Budget, which is introduced at any time between the middle of March and the middle of April according to the government's convenience. The accepted official mode of thinking about the Budget's role in macroeconomic policy has not changed a great deal in the last thirty years. The purpose is to reduce prospective aggregate demand in the economy if it is considered likely to be excessive, or to increase it if it is likely to be deficient. Chancellors have normally presented their Budgets in these terms, explaining at Budget time whether they consider it necessary to stimulate or restrain the economy. It should be noted that by the time the Budget is presented the expenditure estimates for the coming financial year have normally been settled; the items which are varied in the Budget are on the side of tax or revenue rather than expenditure.

There is thus an annual fiscal 'intervention' in the economy at Budget time. The other main group of interventions in British postwar economic history have been those which have taken place quite often in July or August (a time when sterling tends to be seasonally weak) and have been triggered by a balance of payments crisis which has shown itself in a run on the gold and foreign currency reserves. These interventions have tended to be 'packages', which have often included public expenditure cuts, increases in Bank rate and changes in indirect taxation. The purpose of these packages of measures has been not so much to make some carefully calculated adjustment to the movement of demand in the home economy, but rather to reassure foreign holders of sterling.

On the tax side, the instruments have changed quite considerably during the postwar period, particularly in the field of indirect taxation. In the early 1960s, for example, it was decided that the economy needed more instruments that could be effectively used between annual Budgets, so the 'regulator' was introduced, by which a large group of indirect taxes can be raised or lowered by anything up to 10 per cent. The 10 per cent, it should be noted, is a percentage of the previous rate: for example, if the regulator is brought into full operation to increase taxes, a 25 per cent purchase tax rate would be raised to a 27.5 per cent rate. Then in 1966 the government introduced the selective employment tax; this was essentially a tax on employment in services and construction, and it included a premium on employment in manufacturing industry. The most recent major change was the introduction of VAT in 1973, to replace both purchase tax and the selective employment tax. In the field of direct taxation, the main changes have been in corporation tax.

The government has at its disposal a very large number of different fiscal instruments — if one includes in this category not only the various forms of tax, but also all the various forms of subsidy, transfer and benefit. These were the instruments used both for regional policy and, of course, for the redistribution of incomes. By the end of the period, there was a very large number of different types of transfer, benefit and tax, some at national and some at local level, and with a means test applied to some of the benefits. One consequence was that, after the rapid inflation at the end of the period covered in this book, families could find themselves both paying tax and receiving benefit. Another consequence of the means-tested benefits was that some of the low paid found that increases in their gross incomes which took them over the means-test limits could bring about an actual drop in their net disposable income.

On the expenditure side there was a change in doctrine — much more than a change in actual practice — in the early 1960s. An influential committee then recommended that government expenditure should be planned ahead on a five-year basis, and this committee was highly critical of the use of government expenditure as a short-term conjunctural instrument. It argued that this led to great inefficiency and waste, and that in any case expenditure cuts — or for that matter short-term increases in expenditure — usually took much longer to become effective than the government intended. However, although the government in theory accepted this critique of short-term expenditure adjustments, the practice nevertheless remained common throughout the period. Particularly in the packages of measures, which were essentially designed to impress foreign opinion, it continued to be considered more or less obligatory to include some measures reducing public expenditure. The evidence is that in a number of cases the cuts were not particularly effective; they were perhaps valued more for their pronouncement effect than for the reduction in real demand which they brought about.

Monetary policy in Britain has essentially been secondary to fiscal policy. Certainly in the early period up to 1950 the Labour government used it very little; they argued, for example, that since they had direct control of large sectors of investment through the Capital Issues Committee and through building licences, they had no need to use the rate of interest for this purpose. Consequently Bank rate during this early Labour government was hardly used at all. The Conservative government which followed declared itself to be more interested in the use of monetary policy; however, through the bulk of this period the main concern of the Bank of England — certainly so far as medium-term and long-term rates of interest were concerned — was to keep an orderly market so that there could be smooth management of the national debt. Throughout the period the main weapons of monetary policy were non-traditional ones; over the greater part of the period there was some form of direct control over bank advances and the banks were given directives about the type of business which they should favour — such as exports or import-saving projects — and the types of expenditure which they should discourage — such as personal borrowing, or borrowing for property development or for speculative purposes. The other main instrument which was used in the monetary field was also non-traditional; it was the use of hire purchase controls. The government varied the proportion of the total sum borrowed which had to be put down in cash, and also varied the length of the total period over which the borrower had to repay the full sum. The use of this particular instrument also came under heavy criticism on the grounds that it discriminated heavily against particular consumer goods industries, and indeed served to raise costs and prices in those industries; none the less the government has found it so useful an instrument, particularly in its quick effect on consumers' expenditure, that it has been unable to give it up entirely.

The method of control of the banks — and particularly the direct control of bank advances — led to the rapid growth of secondary money markets during this period; the traditional clearing banks began to lose their share of the total provision of credit. Partly for this reason, towards the end of the period an attempt was made to get rid of the direct controls, and to develop a system by which the control was indirect and in which the banks were free to compete against each other. Further, the practice of regular intervention by the Bank of England to prevent any substantial movements in the medium-term or long-term rates of interest was heavily modified. At the end of the period, therefore, the instrument the government was using to influence the supply of credit was no longer the direct control of bank advances, but the requirement on banks to deposit certain sums with the Bank of England — a requirement which could be appropriately varied.

Monetary instruments, therefore, were essentially adjuncts to fiscal instruments in British economic policy throughout this period. Further, on the whole, British governments did not think in terms of a specific objective for the money supply. They calculated in the annual Budget what adjustments were needed to the economy on the basis of forecasts of real flows, and monetary policy was essentially accommodating. There were only one or two occasions when Chancellors of the Exchequer indicated any kind of money supply target; one of the more important instances was when the IMF representatives pressed the government to do so, at a time when Britain had substantial drawings outstanding from the fund.[1]

There are two other general comments to make on the types of instruments which were used: the first concerns exchange rates, and the second concerns the setting up of new institutions. Throughout most of this period, the exchange rate was an instrument of last resort; in the postwar period up to 1970, it was only used twice. Indeed, during most of the period it could more properly be regarded as an objective of economic policy, rather than as an instrument; certainly from 1964 to 1967 it would be right to say that a very large part of economic policy was directed to the defence of the exchange rate. The situation changed with the move to a floating exchange rate in July 1972; from then on it was open to the government, within limits, to manage the movement of the exchange rate, and so to use it to a limited extent as an instrument of economic policy.

Finally, economic policy is not just concerned with the operation of the traditional policy instruments; economic policy makers during the postwar period have spent an appreciable part of their time in devising and establishing new institutions of one kind or another. Indeed this was probably increasingly true throughout the postwar period. As the following sections make clear, governments in their anti-inflation policy began during the 1960s to give less prominence to demand management and more prominence to institutional change; so from 1960 onwards the history of anti-inflation policy is quite largely the history of the attempts to devise effective incomes policy institutions. In much the same way, new institutions were also set up in the hope that they would serve to stimulate Britain's rate of economic growth — first, the National Economic Development Council, then the Department of Economic Affairs, with the National Plan and, at much the same time, the Industrial Reorganization Corporation, in an attempt to increase British industrial efficiency by promoting mergers where considered desirable. It is, of course, much more difficult to evaluate the effects of institutional change than it is to evaluate the effects

---

[1]The target favoured by the IMF was actually domestic credit expansion, which can be defined as the increase in the money supply *plus* the current and capital balance of payments deficit or *minus* the current and capital balance of payments surplus. However, by 1971 when there was a balance of payments surplus, the authorities indicated that domestic credit expansion was no longer in their view an appropriate indicator; from 1971 such official references as there have been to monetary targets have concerned the money supply.

of the operation of some well established instrument of policy; for this reason institutional changes tend sometimes to be omitted from analyses, and indeed from descriptions, of economic policy. They none the less constitute a very important part of the whole.

3. The Use of Policy Instruments

It is perhaps useful to describe first a typical 'policy cycle' in Britain; secondly to describe also some of the policy attempts to break out of this cyclical pattern.

We can begin the description of the policy cycle at the end of a period of stagnation, say, at the end of 1958 or 1962. The trigger for government action is usually that it becomes disturbed about the rising figure for unemployment; it then takes steps to stimulate demand — by removing restrictions on consumer credit (as in 1958), or by tax reductions, or by public expenditure changes. There are, however, a number of time lags before these measures become effective; consequently, it may often appear that the first 'injection' of purchasing power is not working. As a result there may be a slight panic and the government will move to pull out more stops, perhaps with encouragement to nationalized industries or local authorities to accelerate their spending plans.

Eventually the stimulus will take hold; output will begin to rise and, after a lag, unemployment will begin to fall. The first signs of a revival in private investment will appear in manufacturers' declarations of their investment intentions; however, the actual turning point in private investment expenditure is probably some way off.

Within a year the first signs will begin to appear of a worsening in the balance of payments. In the early months when this is happening it may well be that the gold and foreign currency reserves do not fall, since some of the countries with whom we are increasing our trade deficit allow their own reserves to be built up in the form of sterling balances. Then at some point along the road —quite often in the summer, which is usually an unfavourable time of the year for sterling — there is a speculative run against sterling. This, in the fixed exchange rate period, forced the government to take severe deflationary action, which it normally did in the form of a 'package' of measures; this package tended not to be carefully constructed, but rather a hasty collection of measures which, it was hoped, would restore confidence among foreign bankers. So the boom would be brought to an end. There were normally other factors, as well as the imposition of government restraints, which served to slow down the rise in output. Supply side constraints would be beginning to appear, since the economy had moved closer to full capacity working. On the demand side, the peak figure for stockbuilding would probably have been reached, and from then on there would be no further demand stimulus from that source. So it happened on more than one occasion that government restraints were imposed on an economy where the rise in output was already slowing down.

At this point in the policy cycle the period of relative stagnation in output begins; after a time lag unemployment begins to rise. With the very slow rise in output, there is also a slowing down in the rise in the volume of imports. Again after a time lag, the increase in private investment is checked and reversed. The balance of payments gradually moves back into surplus, and the stage is set for the next episode of policy-induced expansion.

4. Attempts to Break the Pattern

The course of postwar economic policy can be seen both as a repetition of the pattern described above, and as a series of attempts to break out of the pattern; these attempts are very briefly described here.

Beginning in the 1960s, a number of new institutional devices were tried in an attempt to raise the underlying growth-rate of the British economy. One of the ideas behind the attempt was that, if a sufficient number of major industrialists could be persuaded that a faster growth-rate was indeed likely, then they would undertake the investment programmes which would make this more rapid growth-rate possible. So the indicative plans contained both in the early work of the National Economic Development Council and in the later work of the Department of Economic Affairs incorporated a significant acceleration of past growth-rates. Another arm of this policy was the increased industrial intervention on the part of the Labour government; the policy comprised both the encouragement of certain mergers through the Industrial Reorganization Corporation, and subsidies and other forms of assistance at the frontiers of technology. These various institutional experiments were unsuccessful in making any radical change in Britain's economic growth-rate and the idea of national planning fell into general disrepute.

At about the same time — that is during the 1960s — experiments were also being made with new institutions to deal with the chronic problem of inflation. The Conservative government in the early 1960s came to the conclusion that demand management was an unsuccessful method of dealing with inflationary problems and, towards the end of its period of office, the National Incomes Commission was set up. It had a rather short life; it had few powers and no trade union support; it disappeared with the end of the Conservative government in October 1964.

The second institutional attempt to deal with this problem was that of the Labour government. They initiated their incomes policy with a Statement of Intent, signed by representatives of the TUC, the CBI and the government. The basic principle was that of a 'norm' for wage increases, in line with the expected increase in output. Observance of this norm was, essentially, to be voluntary, but the government also established the National Board for Prices and Incomes, which was empowered to deal with references made to it by the government — both on prices and on incomes. However, it only had powers of delay. The policy proved to be a fairly weak one, and it went through a number of vicissitudes during the Labour government's years. For a while the TUC set up its own vetting committee for wage claims; then — after one of the sterling crises which preoccupied the government in this period — there was a wages and prices freeze for six months from mid-1966. The freeze was followed by a period of 'severe restraint', but here again the only power the government possessed was the power of postponement of a wage award on the recommendation of the National Board for Prices and Incomes. In the final period of incomes policy, a good deal of emphasis was given to productivity agreements as justifiable exceptions from the basic 'norm', and a great many awards were dressed up as productivity agreements. By 1969 the government was coming to the conclusion that the potentialities of incomes policy were more or less exhausted and the focus of attention was shifted to the problem of unofficial strikes. It was decided that it might be a more promising approach to find ways of outlawing unofficial strikes; it was therefore proposed to introduce a bill to reform industrial relations. This was faced with such strong opposition from the TUC and from the Labour Party itself that the government was forced to drop this legislation in exchange for a 'solemn and binding' agreement that the TUC would do something about the problem.

The Conservative government came to power in mid-1970

opposed to any form of formal incomes policy. It abolished the National Board for Prices and Incomes. It also proceeded to attempt to bring the trade unions 'within the framework of the law' by an Industrial Relations Act; at the same time it was careful to avoid any vigorous reflationary action to bring unemployment down, and in the public sector it pursued a policy which became known as the 'N−1' policy, under which it attempted to ensure that each successive settlement was 1 per cent lower than the previous one. This policy in effect broke up early in 1972. First of all, the government failed to hold unemployment even at the relatively high level it inherited; right through 1971 unemployment rose rapidly, to pass the million mark in early 1972, yet it seemed to have little effect in moderating the size of wage awards. Secondly, the policy of bringing down the size of settlements in the public sector was broken by the miners' strike in early 1972, which in effect forced a government capitulation.

In 1972, therefore, the Conservative government changed its strategy, and made another attempt to break out into a sustained period of faster growth. This strategy included an expansionary Budget, to bring down the rate of unemployment and to give a demand stimulus to investment; it also included a move to a floating exchange rate in mid-1972, in the hope that this would effectively remove the balance of payments constraint on economic growth; the third element in the strategy was the determination to reintroduce some kind of incomes policy. The government attempted in the middle of 1972 to reach a consensus agreement with the trade union leaders, but failed; and in November it adopted a statutory prices and incomes policy. The intention of this combination of policies was to bring about a 5 per cent growth-rate, which the government hoped might persist, combined with a moderate price rise and a balance of payments outcome, which would, as it were, be protected by the falling exchange rate.

This combination of policies did not bring the hoped-for breakthrough into longer-term faster growth. It is true that in the short term the rise in national output did accelerate during 1972 and early 1973, and in its first and second stages the new statutory incomes policy survived the opposition of the trade union movement. However, although the exchange rate fell, a very substantial balance of payments deficit emerged, which showed no signs of disappearing. This was partly because this particular 'dash for growth' unfortunately coincided with a world commodity price boom, culminating in the trebling of oil prices over the winter of

1973-4. By the middle of 1974 total import prices (in sterling terms) had doubled from their level in 1972.

Finally, the third stage of the Conservative government's incomes policy encountered a miners' strike in the early months of 1974; a general election was called, the Conservative Party failed to get a majority and was succeeded by a Labour government. It is hard to assess as yet how far the Conservative government's strategy was essentially misguided, or how far its failure to accelerate the underlying growth-rate was due to an unfortunate set of international circumstances.

The Labour government came into power in February 1974 at the beginning of a world recession. It abandoned the statutory approach to incomes policy; however, throughout 1974 the provisions of the Conservative government's Stage III policy were still serving to accelerate the rise in wage rates. For this policy, conceived before the increase in oil prices at the end of 1973, provided for full compensation in wage rates for any increase in prices which exceeded 7 per cent from the base date in October 1973. By April 1974 this threshold had been passed, and this provision of the Conservative government's incomes policy continued to push up both wages and prices throughout 1974.

The Labour government's approach to incomes policy was to persuade the trade unions to subscribe to a loosely worded declaration that they intended to be moderate in their wage demands — a declaration called the 'social contract'. The provisions were so imprecise, however, that by the middle of 1975 average earnings were some 28 per cent, and retail prices some 25 per cent, higher than a year earlier. While the rate of inflation was moving rapidly up in this way, national output was falling and unemployment was rising sharply.

In July 1975, the trade union movement initiated and agreed to a much stricter form of incomes policy, with a uniform limit of a £6 per week increase for everyone, except for those earning £8,500 a year or more who were to have no increase at all. At the time of writing (March 1976) this policy was having some success in bringing down the rate of increase in both earnings and retail prices. At this time the government's longer-term policies were still in their formative stage.

*   *   *   *   *

Behind the phrase 'management of the British economy' there lies a certain concept of economic policy: that, by the operation of fiscal, monetary or exchange rate instruments, the government can bring about a reasonable degree of improvement in the performance of the economy. Indeed, in the 1950s, 'management' was mainly conceived as a set of monetary or fiscal adjustments which reduced demand when it was considered to be too high, or increased it when it was considered to be too low. These adjustments were essentially short-term.

Increasingly during the 1960s and 1970s policy makers were coming to the conclusion that demand regulation was not enough; it did not carry with it the solution to the problems of inflation, or inadequate economic growth, or chronic difficulties with the balance of payments. So new, longer-term policies began to come to the fore, concerned with attempts to bring about some form of structural change. Thus from 1962 onwards there were successive experiments with various forms of incomes policy, involving to a greater or lesser extent radical changes in the form of bargaining about wages. There were experiments with planning, both under Conservative and under Labour governments, but, as a consequence of the apparent failure of national economic planning in the period 1964-9, the Labour government which came to power in 1974 was more concerned with finding ways of reaching agreements with individual firms, particularly on investment plans. There was increasing recognition in studies of various industries that British lack of success seemed to be more connected with failures in management–worker relations. The general implication was that 'macroeconomic' intervention was not enough; the government had to intervene at a 'microeconomic' level as well.

There was also at this time an opposite reaction — though, at the time of writing (May 1977) this had not been embodied into the actual policy of any government — that the government, instead of increasing the area of its intervention, should rather move to reduce the scope of its 'demand management'. It should restrict itself to adhering to some simple rule, such as a money supply rule or a 'size of budget deficit' rule. Whether the long-term trend of economic policy towards more intervention is likely to be reversed for any length of time remains to be seen.

BIBLIOGRAPHY

Periodicals

	Chapter[1]
(a) *Government*[2]	
Ministry of Agriculture, Fisheries and Food,	
Annual Review	2
Central Statistical Office, *Abstract of Regional Statistics*	
(annual)	Gen.
Annual Abstract of Statistics	Gen.
Economic Trends (monthly)	Gen.
Financial Statistics (monthly)	5
Monthly Digest of Statistics	Gen.
National Income and Expenditure (annual)	Gen.
Social Trends (annual)	3
United Kingdom Balance of Payments (annual)	Gen.
Customs and Excise, *Report of the Commissioners*	
(annual)	4
Department of Education and Science, *Education*	
Statistics for the United Kingdom (annual)	3
Statistics of Education. England and Wales, vols. 1-6	
(annual)	3
Department of Employment, *British Labour Statistics*	
Yearbook	Gen.
Family Expenditure Survey (annual)	3
Gazette (monthly)	Gen.
Department of the Environment, *Housing and*	
Construction Statistics (quarterly)	3
Department of Health and Social Security, *Annual Report*	3
Digest of Health Statistics for England and Wales	
(annual)	3

---

[1]Publications marked 'Gen.' in this column are the principal statistical sources of general relevance to the British economy; the others refer particularly to the Chapters in this volume as shown.

[2]All the government periodicals are published in London by HM Stationery Office unless otherwise stated.

Department of Industry, *Business Monitor: overseas
 transactions* (miscellaneous series M4) (annual)   6
  Business Monitor: report on the Census of Production
   (series PA) (annual)   2
Inland Revenue, *Report of the Commissioners* (annual)   4
Northern Ireland Registrar General, *Annual Report,*
 Belfast   1
Office of Population Censuses and Surveys, *Census of
 Population: England and Wales* (5-yearly)   3
  *Registrar General's Quarterly Return for England
   and Wales*   1
  *Registrar General's Statistical Review of England and
   Wales* (annual)   1
Scotland Registrar General, *Annual Report,* Edinburgh   1
Department of Trade, *Trade and Industry* (weekly)   Gen.
Treasury, *Financial Statement and Budget Report* (annual)   4

(b) *Other*
Bank of England Quarterly Bulletin   Gen.[1]
British Airports Authority, *Annual Report and Accounts*   4
British Airways, *Annual Report and Accounts*   4
British Gas Corporation, *Annual Report and Accounts*   4
British Journal of Industrial Relations (4-monthly)   3
British Railways Board, *Annual Report and Accounts*   4
British Steel Corporation, *Annual Report and Accounts*   4
Central Electricity Generating Board, *Annual Report and
 Accounts* (also *Reports* from the regional Boards)   4
Electricity Council, *Statement of Accounts and Statistics*
 (annual)   4
Incomes Data Service (fortnightly)   3
Industrial Relations Journal (quarterly)   3
Industrial Relations Review and Report (fortnightly)   3
National Bus Company, *Report and Accounts* (annual)   4
National Coal Board, *Report and Accounts* (annual)   4
National Institute Economic Review (quarterly)   Gen.[2]
Trades Union Congress, *Annual Report*   3

[1]In addition to regular analyses of the whole economy, this contains a
number of special articles particularly relevant to Chapters 5 and 6.

[2]In addition to regular analyses of the whole economy, this contains a
number of special articles particularly relevant to Chapters 6 and 7.

Other Official Publications

(a) *United Kingdom government* [1]

Cabinet Office, *The United Kingdom and the European Communities,* Cmnd 4715, 1971	6
Central Office of Information, *Social Security in Britain* (2nd ed.), 1973	3
Britain 1977: an official handbook, 1977	Gen.
Department of Economic Affairs, *The National Plan,* Cmnd 2764, 1965	7
Investment Incentives, Cmnd 2874, 1966	4
The Intermediate Areas (Hunt Report), Cmnd 3889, 1969	1
Department of Employment (and Productivity), *In Place of Strife: a policy for industrial relations,* Cmnd 3888, 1969	3
British Labour Statistics: historical abstract 1886-1968, 1971	1,3
Department of the Environment, *Future Shape of Local Government Finance,* Cmnd 4741, 1971	4
Foreign Office, *Report on the Geneva Tariff Negotiations 1960-62,* Cmnd 1804, 1962	6
House of Commons, *First Report from the Select Committee on Nationalized Industries. Bank of England,* HC258, 1970	5
Report of the Select Committee on Corporation Tax, HC622, 1971	4
Select Committee on Tax Credit. Report and proceedings, HC341, 1973	4
Select Committee on Nationalized Industries. First report: capital investment procedures, HC65, 1974	4
Ministry of Housing and Local Government, *Report of the Committee of Inquiry into the Impact of Rates on Households* (Allen Report), Cmnd 2582, 1965	4
Local Government Finance. England and Wales, Cmnd 2923, 1966	4
Inland Revenue, *Report of the Committee on Turnover Taxation* (Richardson Report), Cmnd 2300, 1964	4

[1] All published in London by HM Stationery Office unless otherwise stated.

Ministry of Labour, *Employment Policy*, Cmd 6527,
 1944   1
National Board for Prices and Incomes, *Report No. 34.*
 Bank Charges, Cmnd 3292, 1967   5
National Economic Development Council, *Export Trends,*
 1963   6
 Investment Appraisal, 1965   4
National Economic Development Office, *Value Added*
 Tax, 1969
 The Measurement and Interpretation of Service Output
 Changes by A.D. Smith, London, NEDO, 1972   2
Office of Population Censuses and Surveys, *General*
 Household Survey: introductory report, 1973   3
Royal Commission on the Distribution of the Industrial
 Population, *Report* (Barlow Report), Cmd 6153, 1939   1
Royal Commission on Trade Unions and Employers'
 Associations, *Report* (Donovan Report), Cmnd 3623,
 1968 (and Research Papers 1-11)   3
Board of Trade, *European Free Trade Association,* Cmnd
 906, 1959   6
 The Kennedy Round of Trade Negotiations, 1964-67,
 Cmnd 3347, 1967   6
 The Movement of Manufacturing Industry in the United
 Kingdom, 1945-65, 1968   1
Department of Trade and Industry, *Report of the*
 Committee on Consumer Credit (Crowther Report),
 Cmnd 4596, 1971   5
Treasury, *Committee on the Working of the Monetary*
 System. Report (Radcliffe Report), Cmnd 827, 1959   5
 United Kingdom Balance of Payments, 1946-57, 1959   6
 The Financial and Economic Obligations of the
 Nationalized Industries, Cmnd 1337, 1961   4
 Control of Public Expenditure. Report (Plowden
 Report), Cmnd 1432, 1961   4
 Taxation of Short-term Gains, Cmnd 1710, 1962   4
 Taxation of Capital Gains, Cmnd 2645, 1965   4
 Corporation Tax, Cmnd 2646, 1965   4
 Selective Employment Tax, Cmnd 2986, 1966   4
 Nationalized Industries: a review of economic and
 financial objectives, Cmnd 3437, 1967   4
 Public Expenditure: a new presentation, Cmnd 4017,
 1969   4

Ministerial Control of the Nationalized Industries, Cmnd 4027, 1969	4
Public Expenditure 1968-69 to 1973-74, Cmnd 4234, 1969 (and annually thereafter)	4
Effects of the Selective Employment Tax. First report: the distributive trades (Reddaway Report), 1970	2,4
Investment Incentives, Cmnd 4516, 1970	4
Value-added Tax (Green Paper), Cmnd 4621, 1971	4
Reform of Corporation Tax (Green Paper), Cmnd 4630, 1971	4
Reform of Personal Direct Taxation, Cmnd 4653, 1971	4
Value Added Tax (White Paper), Cmnd 4929, 1972	4
Taxation of Capital on Death. Possible inheritance tax in place of estate duty, Cmnd 4930, 1972	4
Reform of Corporation Tax (White Paper), Cmnd 4955, 1972	4
Proposals for a Tax-credit System, Cmnd 5116, 1972	4
Public Expenditure White Papers: handbook on methodology, 1972	4
Wealth Tax, Cmnd 5704, 1974	4
Capital Transfer Tax, Cmnd 5705, 1974	4

(b) *International bodies*

European Communities, Monetary Committee, *Monetary Policy in the Countries of the EEC,* Supplement: *The United Kingdom*, Geneva, 1974	5
International Monetary Fund, 'The short-run effects of domestic demand pressure on British export performance' by J.R. Artus, *IMF Staff Papers,* vol. 17, July 1970	6
Organization for Economic Cooperation and Development, *The Measurement of Real Product: a theoretical and empirical analysis of the growth rates for different industries and countries* by T.P. Hill, Paris, 1971	2
Revenue Statistics of the OECD Member Countries, 1965-74, Paris, 1976	4

Books and Articles

D.H. Aldcroft and P. Fearon, *Economic Growth in
    Twentieth-Century Britain,* London, Macmillan, 1969   Gen.
G.C. Archibald, 'Analysis of regional economic policy' in
    M. Peston and B.A. Corry (eds.), *Essays in Honour of
    Lord Robbins,* London, Weidenfeld and Nicolson,
    1972   1
A. Armstrong and A. Silberston, 'Size of plant, size of
    enterprise and concentration in British manufacturing
    industry 1935-58', *Journal of the Royal Statistical
    Society* (series A), vol. 128, 1965   2
Michael Artis, *Foundations of British Monetary Policy,*
    Oxford, Basil Blackwell, 1965   5
A.D. Bain, *The Control of the Money Supply,* London,
    Penguin Books, 1970   5
R.J. Ball, J.R. Eaton and M.D. Steuer, 'The relationship
    between UK export performance in manufactures and
    the internal pressure of demand', *Economic Journal,*
    vol. 76, September 1966   6
T.S. Barker and J.R.C. Lecomber, 'The import content
    of final expenditures for the United Kingdom
    1954-1972', *Bulletin of the Oxford University Institute
    of Economics and Statistics,* vol. 32, February 1970   6
W. Beckerman (ed.), *The Labour Government's Economic
    Record, 1964-1970,* London, Duckworth, 1972   Gen.
W. Beckerman and Associates, *The British Economy in
    1975*, Cambridge University Press, 1965   Gen.
P.W. Bell, *The Sterling Area in the Postwar World:
    internal mechanism and cohesion, 1946-1952,* Oxford,
    Clarendon Press, 1956   6
F.T. Blackaby, *British Share of World Trade in
    Manufactures,* London, Woolwich Polytechnic, 1965   6
John Bowers and V.H. Woodward, 'The anatomy of
    regional activity rates' and 'Regional social accounts for
    the United Kingdom' in *Regional Papers I,* Cambridge
    University Press, 1970   1
A.L. Bowley, *Some Economic Consequences of the Great
    War,* London, Butterworth, 1930   1
S. Brittan, *Steering the Economy: the role of the Treasury*
    (revised ed.) London, Penguin Books, 1971   7
A.J. Brown, 'Surveys of applied economics: regional

economics with special reference to the United
Kingdom', *Economic Journal,* vol. 79, December 1969[1]
  *The Framework of Regional Economics in the United
  Kingdom,* Cambridge University Press, 1972 1
J. Bruce-Gardyne, *Whatever Happened to the Quiet
Revolution?* London, Charles Knight, 1974 7
A. Cairncross (ed.), *Britain's Economic Prospects
Reconsidered,* London, Allen and Unwin, 1970 Gen.
R.E. Caves and Associates, *Britain's Economic Prospects,*
Washington DC, The Brookings Institution, 1968 Gen.
P.C. Cheshire and R. Weeden, 'Regional unemployment
differences in Great Britain' and 'Interregional
migration models and their application to Great Britain'
in *Regional Papers II,* Cambridge University Press, 1973 1
H.A. Clegg, *The System of Industrial Relations in Great
Britain,* Oxford, Basil Blackwell, 1970 3
Committee on Invisible Exports, *Britain's Invisible
Earnings: the report of the Committee on Invisible
Exports,* London, British National Export Council,
1967 6
A.R. Conan, *The Sterling Area,* London, Macmillan, 1952 6
Capital Imports into Sterling Countries, London,
Macmillan, 1960 6
*The Rationale of the Sterling Area: texts and
commentary,* London, Macmillan, 1961 6
The Problem of Sterling, London, Macmillan, 1966 6
R.A. Cooper and K. Hartley, *Export Performance and the
Pressure of Demand: a study of firms,* London, Allen
and Unwin, 1970 6
A.B. Cramp, *Monetary Management: principles and
practice,* London, Allen and Unwin, 1971 5
J.B. Cullingworth and Sarah C. Orr (eds.), *Regional and
Urban Studies: a social science approach,* London,
Allen and Unwin, 1969 1
N.J. Cunningham, 'A note on the "proper distribution of
industry" ', *Oxford Economic Papers,* vol. 21 (new
series), March 1969 1
A.C.L. Day, *The Economics of Money,* London, Oxford
University Press, 1959 5

[1]A comprehensive bibliography on regional problems, relevant to
Chapter 1, section 4 of this book, is given at the end of this article.

B.M. Deakin and K.D. George, *Productivity in Transport: a study of employment, capital, output and technical change,* Cambridge University Press, 1969   2

P.M. Deane and W.A. Cole, *British Economic Growth 1688-1959,* Cambridge University Press, 1962   6

J.G.S. Donaldson, F. Donaldson and B. Barber, *Farming in Britain Today,* London, Allen Lane, 1969   2

J.C.R. Dow, *The Management of the British Economy, 1945-60,* Cambridge University Press, 1963   Gen.

O. Eckstein, F.T. Blackaby and J. Faaland, *Economic Policy in Our Time,* vol. II, *Country Studies,* Amsterdam, North-Holland, 1964   7

Economist Intelligence Unit, *The Commonwealth and Europe,* London, Whitefriars Press, 1960   6

R.W. Evely and I.M.D. Little, *Concentration in British Industry,* Cambridge University Press, 1960   2

A. Fels, *The Prices and Incomes Board,* Cambridge University Press, 1972   7

C.D. Foster, *Politics, Finance and the Role of Economics: an essay on the control of public enterprise,* London, Allen and Unwin, 1971   4

K.D. George, *Productivity in Distribution,* Cambridge University Press, 1966   2

'The changing structure of competitive industry', *Economic Journal,* vol. 82 (supplement), 1972   2

Andrew Glyn and Bob Sutcliffe, *British Capitalism, Workers and the Profits Squeeze,* Harmondsworth, Penguin Books, 1972   7

M. Hall, J. Knapp and C. Winsten, *Distribution in Great Britain and North America,* London, Oxford University Press, 1961   2

R.F. Harrod, *The British Economy,* London, McGraw-Hill, 1963   6

P.E. Hart and S.J. Prais, 'The analysis of business concentration: a statistical approach,' *Journal of the Royal Statistical Society* (series A), vol. 119, part 2, 1956   2

P.E. Hart, M.A. Utton and G. Walshe, *Mergers and Concentration in British Industry,* Cambridge University Press, 1973   2

M.F.W. Hemming and W.M. Corden, 'Import restriction as an instrument of balance-of-payments policy', *Economic Journal,* vol. 68, September 1958   6

M.F.W. Hemming, C. Miles and G.F. Ray, 'A statistical
summary of the extent of import control in the United
Kingdom since the war', *Review of Economic Studies,*
vol. 26, February 1959   6

P.D. Henderson (ed.), *Economic Growth in Britain,*
London, Weidenfeld and Nicolson, 1966   7

M. Howe, 'British merger policy proposals and American
experience', *Scottish Journal of Political Economy,*
vol. 19, February 1972   2

T. E. Josling, *Agriculture and Britain's Trade Policy
Dilemma,* London, Trade Policy Research Centre, 1970   6

C.P. Kindleberger, 'Foreign trade and growth: lessons
from British experience since 1913', *Lloyds Bank
Review,* no. 65, July 1962   6

The World in Depression 1929-1939, London, Allen Lane, 1973   6

C.H. Lee, *Regional Economic Development in the United
Kingdom since the 1880s,* Maidenhead, McGraw-Hill,
1971   1

London and Cambridge Economic Service, *Key Statistics
of the British Economy 1900-1970,* London, Times,
1971.   6

W.F. Luttrell, *Factory Location and Industrial
Movement: a study of recent experience in Great
Britain,* London, National Institute of Economic and
Social Research, 1962   1

G. McCrone, *Regional Policy in Britain,* London, Allen
and Unwin, 1969   1

C.W. McMahon, *Sterling in the Sixties,* London, Oxford
University Press, 1964   6

A. Maizels, *Industrial Growth and World Trade,*
Cambridge University Press, 1963   6

R.C.O. Matthews, 'Some aspects of postwar growth in the
British economy in relation to historical experience',
paper read to the Manchester Statistical Society, 1964   2

'Foreign trade and British economic growth', *Scottish
Journal of Political Economy,* vol. 20, November 1973   6

Joan Mitchell, *Groundwork of Economic Planning,*
London, Secker and Warburg, 1966   7

D.E. Moggeridge, *British Monetary Policy 1924-1931:
the Norman Conquest of $4.86,* Cambridge University
Press, 1972   6

G. Myrdal, *Challenge to Affluence,* London, Gollancz, 1963   1

National Institute of Economic and Social Research,
'The effects of the devaluation of 1967 on the current
balance of payments', *Economic Journal,* vol. 82,
March 1972   6

L. Needleman (ed.), *Regional Analysis,* Harmondsworth,
Penguin Books, 1968   1

D.J. O'Dea, *Cyclical Indicators for the Postwar British
Economy,* Cambridge University Press, 1975   1

F.W. Paish, *How the Economy Works and Other Essays,*
London, Macmillan, 1970   7

J.R. Parkinson, 'The progress of United Kingdom
exports', *Scottish Journal of Political Economy,* vol. 13,
February 1966   6

J.O.N. Perkins, *The Sterling Area, the Commonwealth
and World Economic Growth* (2nd ed.), C.U.P., 1970   6

M.V. Posner, *Fuel Policy: a study in applied economics,*
London, Macmillan, 1973   4

S.J. Prais, *The Evolution of Giant Firms in Britain,*
Cambridge University Press, 1976   2

C.F. Pratten, *Economies of Scale in Manufacturing
Industry,* Cambridge University Press, 1971   2

A.R. Prest and D.J. Coppock (eds.), *The UK Economy:
a manual of applied economics,* London, Weidenfeld and
Nicolson, 1972   1,2

R. Pryke, *Public Enterprise in Practice,* London,
MacGibbon and Kee, 1971   4

W.B. Reddaway, *Effects of the Selective Employment
Tax. Final report,* Cambridge University Press, 1973   2,4

J. Revell, *Changes in British Banking: the growth of a
secondary banking system,* London, Hill Samuel, 1968   5

J. Rhodes and A. Kan, *Office Dispersal and Regional
Policy,* Cambridge University Press, 1971   1

H.W. Richardson, *Regional Economics: location theory,
urban structure and regional change,* London,
Weidenfeld and Nicolson, 1969   1

C.K. Rowley, *The British Monopolies Commission,*
London, Allen and Unwin, 1967   2
'Mergers and public policy in Great Britain', *Journal of
Law and Economics,* vol. 11, April 1968   2

M.C. Sawyer, 'Concentration in British manufacturing
industry', *Oxford Economic Papers,* vol. 23 (new
series), November 1971   2

R.S. Sayers, *Modern Banking* (7th ed.) Oxford,
    Clarendon Press, 1967   5

M.FG. Scott, *A Study of United Kingdom Imports,*
    Cambridge University Press, 1963   6

A. Singh, *Takeovers, their Relevance to the Stock Market and
    the Theory of the Firm,* Cambridge University Press, 1971   2

R.B. Stevens and B.S. Yamey, *The Restrictive Practices
    Court,* London, Weidenfeld and Nicolson, 1966   2

R. Stone and T.S. Barker, *The Determinants of Britain's
    Visible Imports 1949-1966,* London, Chapman & Hall, 1970   6

A. Sutherland, *The Monopolies Commission in Action,*
    Cambridge University Press, 1969   2

D. Swann, D.P. O'Brien, W.P. Maunder and W.S.
    Howe, *Competition in British Industry: restrictive
    practices legislation in theory and practice,* London
    Allen and Unwin, 1974   2

L. Tivey (ed.), *The Nationalized Industries since 1960.
    A book of readings,* London, Allen and Unwin, 1973   4

R. Triffin, *The Fate of the Pound,* Paris, Atlantic Inst., 1969   6

M.A. Utton, 'The effect of mergers on concentration: UK
    manufacturing industry 1954-65', *Journal of Industrial
    Economics,* vol. 20, November 1971   2

G. Walshe, *Recent Trends in Monopoly in Great Britain,*
    Cambridge University Press, 1974   2

T.S. Ward, *The Distribution of Consumer Goods:
    structure and performance,* C.U.P., 1973   2

B. Wasserstein, 'British merger policy from an American
    perspective', *Yale Law Journal,* vol. 83, March 1973   2

A.E. Webb and R. Weeden, 'Unemployment, vacancies
    and the rate of change of earnings' and 'Regional rates
    of employment growth' in *Regional Papers III,*
    Cambridge University Press, 1974   1

K.W. Wedderburn, *The Worker and the Law,*
    Harmondsworth, Penguin Books, 1965   3

S.J. Wells, *British Export Performance: a comparative
    study,* Cambridge University Press, 1964   6

Harold Wilson, *The Labour Government 1964-1970,*
    London, Weidenfeld and Michael Joseph, 1971   7

G.D.N. Worswick and P.H. Ady (eds.), *The British
    Economy 1945-1950,* Oxford, Clarendon Press, 1952   Gen.
    The British Economy in the Nineteen-Fifties, Oxford,
    Clarendon Press, 1962   Gen.

INDEX

The letter-by-letter system of alphabetization has been adopted; acronyms have been freely used: thus the CONfederation of British Industries, will be found under CBI.

abortion laws and demography, 8
ACAS, 55
age:
  raising of school-leaving, 57
  yearly table of population composition by, 9-11
agricultural interests, 4
agricultural output, distribution of, 46
agricultural sector discussed, 45-9
agriculture, changes in methods of, 14-15
allocation of materials, policy of, 110
allowances, taxation, 70-71
assets, external, 104
AUEW, 50

balance of payments, 86-8, 103
banking, growth of, 14, 42-3
Bank of England, 75, 81, 82, 84, 112
Bank of England Act (1946), 83
bank rate, 83
  see also MLR
banks:
  big four clearing, 76
  secondary, 76-7
Barlow Report (1939), 24
benefits, payment of, 58-9, 111-12
bibliography, 121-32
birth rate, 6-9
Bretton Woods Agreement, 5
bricks, 33
British Savings Bonds, 79
brokerage earnings, 43
brokers, 79
budget, 110-11
building societies, 78

capital balances, 103-6
capital expenditure and employment figures, table of, 31-2
capital funds for industry and commerce, 80

capital gains tax, 71
Capital Issues Committee, 112
catering industry, 42
CBI, 53
cement, 33
Census of Production, data from, 36
central clearing system (of cheques), 76
chemical industry, 31-3
City, financial earnings of the, 43
clothing industry, 29, 33-4
coal industry, decline of, 4
collective bargaining, standardizing wages through, 20-21, 52-3
colonies, effect of changes in, 5
Commission on Industrial Relations (CIR), 54
Committee on Intermediate Areas (1969), 25
Common Agricultural Policy (CAP), 6, 47, 49
Common External Tariff, 91, 92
Commonwealth Immigrants Act (1962), 8
Commonwealth Preference Area, 5, 88-91
Commonwealth Sugar Agreement, 49, 89
communications, nationalization of, 72-4
concentration of industry, 34-41
conciliation and arbitration, 53, 55
conditions of employment, union negotiations over, 52
construction industry, decline of, 13
consumer durables, increase in expenditure on, 16-17
consumer subsidies, 48, 65-6
contraceptives and demography, 8
Control of Public Expenditure (Plowden Report), 61
corporate tax, 68-9, 111
cotton industry, decline of, 4
craft unions, 50-52
credit control, 81

132

currency notes, issue of, 75
customs duties, 70
see also tariffs

death:
    causes of, 57
    rate, 82
debt management, 82
deficiency payments (to farmers), 48
demography, trends in, 6-13
deposit accounts, control of interest rate on, 85
deposit institutions, 76-8
Depression, the Great, 2-3
devaluation, 101
Development Areas, 24-5, 69, 108-9
Dillon Round, 92
Director General of Fair Trading, 38-41
discount houses, 77, 83, 84
diseases, contraction of infectious, 57
dismissal, unfair, 52, 55
Distribution of Industry Act (1946), 24
dollars:
    pooling of, 89
    rate for, 93-4
Donovan Commission (1964), 53-4

earned income relief, 71
Economic Affairs, Department of, 110, 114, 116
economic regulators, 111
economy:
    general features of, 1-28:
        demography, trends in, 6-13
            employment, 10-13
            population, 6-10
        national product, 13-17
            output of UK, 13-17
        regional differences, 17-27
    management of British, 107-20:
        institutions, 109-15
        instruments, 109-15
        objectives, 107-9
        pattern-breaking (of policy cycle), 116-20
    policy instruments, use of, 115-16
education:
    age of school-leaving and, 10-11
    financing of, 65
    policy for, 57-8
EEC, effects of joining, 47-9, 91

EFTA, 90-91
    see also free trade, policy of
electricity, increase in use of, 14-15, 29
electronics, 30-31
employment:
    demography of, 10-13
    numbers in, in manufacturing, 34
    policy of full, 107-8
    table of, in service industries, 42
    table of regional growth in, 19
    trends in, 10-13
    union negotiations on conditions of, 52
    see also unemployment
Employment, Department of, 52-3
Employment Protection Act (1975), 55
Equal Pay Act (1970), 54
Eurodollars, 76-7, 103
exchange control, 5, 75, 80, 89-90
Exchange Equalization Account, 75, 92, 93
exchange rate:
    policy over, 93-4
    variations in, 114
excise duties, 70
expenditure, comparative table of, 16
exports:
    Britain's share of, 2-3
    changes in area of (1900-76), 100
    payment for, 95-102
external trade, *see* trade, external

Fair Trading Act (1973), 38, 40
family allowances, 59
farms, 46-7
female/male ratio, 8
FFI, 79
finance, *see* financial institutions; monetary policy; public finance
Finance Act (1962), 71
Finance Act (1975), 71
Finance Corporation for Industry, 78
Finance for Industry Ltd., 79
financial institutions, 75-80:
    Bank of England, 75
    control regulations for, 83-5
    deposit institutions, 76-8
    others, 78-9
    sources of investment funds, 79-80
fiscal packages, 111
fiscal policies defined, 110-11
floating rates, 101, 114

133

food:
    advantages of cheap, 4, 33, 47-9
    importation of, 45-8
    origin of imports of, 48
food industry, growth of, 29
footwear industry, 29
free trade, policy of, 3-6, 47
    see also EFTA
Friendly Societies, Registrar of, 78
fringe benefits, 52
fuel industry, nationalization of, 72-4

gas:
    increase in use of, 14-15, 29
    taxation on North Sea, 71-2
GATT, 5, 90, 92
GDP, 13-15, 61
    percentage of industrial production in, 29
    public expenditure as proportion of, 62-4
Geneva Round (1956), 92
gilt-edged market, 82
giro system, 77-8
glass industry, 33
G and MWU, 50
GNP, 66-7
    ratio of tax to, 66-7
gold standard, 4-5
goods and services, 41-9
goods industries, table of productivity in, 44
Gorman, John, 43
government, *see* state
graduates, rise in unemployment of, 12
grievance procedure, 52
growth-rate, comparisons of, 3
    in Britain, 13-15
guaranteed prices (to farmers), 48

Hart and Prais (1956), 34-5
Havana Charter of International Trade, 5
health and safety matters, 52
health and welfare, policy for, 55-7
hire purchase, 77, 85, 113
hotel industry, 42
hours of work, 52
housing:
    investment, 65
    policy, 59-60

illness, 55-7, 58-9
IMF, 5, 92, 105, 113-14
immigrant population, 8
imports:
    changes in composition of (1935-76), 98
    payment for, 95-102
income elasticities, 43
income:
    per capita, 20
    policy, attempts at, 117-19
    policy of redistribution of, 111
    support policy, 58-9
    tax, 70-72
industrial action, 52
Industrial and Commercial Finance Corporation, 78-9
Industrial Development Certificates, 24, 26
industrial production:
    table of inputs, 32
    table of outputs, 30
industrial relations, *see* social issues
Industrial Relations Act (1971), 54, 118
Industrial Reorganization Corporation, 114, 116
industrial sector:
    concentration of, 34-41
    production, 29-34
industrial unions, 51
industry:
    tendency for concentration of, 34-41
    trends in distribution of, 23
inflation, 53, 65-6, 81, 107, 112, 114, 117, 119
In Place of Strife: a Policy for Industrial Relations, 54
instrument engineering, 31
insurance:
    companies, 78
    growth in industry in, 14, 42, 43
    National Scheme, 58-9
interest rate, 81, 85, 113
Intermediate Areas, 25
investment funds, sources of, 79-80
Investment Trusts, 78
invisible earnings, 102-3
iron and steel, nationalization of, 72-4
Issue Department, Bank of England, 75

jobbers, 79

Kennedy Round, 92

labour relations, *see* social issues
laissez-faire, policy of, 3-4
land area used for agriculture, 46
lavatories, indoor, 60
law, trade unions and the, 53-5
leather industry, decline in, 29, 33
lender of last resort, 75, 77, 84
liabilities, external, 104
loans, personal, 76, 77

male/female ratio, 8
management of economy, *see under* economy
manufactures:
    table of exports of, 102
    table of imports of, 96, 98
marine engineering, decline in, 29
means tests, 112
mechanization of agriculture, 47
medical services, 56-7
merchant banks, 43, 76
merger activity, 35-7, 114
metal industry, 29, 31
migration:
    effect on regions of, 22-3
    effects of, on population, 8
Minimum Lending Rate, 82-3
mining industry, changes in, 14-15, 29
MLR, 82-3
monetary policy and mechanisms, 80-85:
    debt management, 82
    financial institutions, regulations for, 83-5
    hire purchase controls, 85
    MLR, 82-3
    Treasury bill market, 82-3
money supply, 81
monopolies, 37-40
Monopolies and Mergers Act (1965), 40
Monopolies Commission, 38-40
mortgages, 78
'most favoured nation' duties, 90, 92
motor industry, 29-30
Musgrave, R. A. and P. B., 63-4

National Board for Prices and Incomes, 74, 117
national debt, 81

National Economic Development Council, 53, 61, 114, 116
National Giro Scheme, 77-8
National Health Service, 55-7, 65
National Incomes Commission, 117
National Industrial Relations Court, 54
National Insurance scheme, 58
nationalized industries:
    public financing of, 72-4
    programme for, 4
National Product, 13-17
national savings, 79
negative income tax, 71
net property income, 103
New Towns policy, 26
NFBTO, 51
N-1 policy, 118
Northern Ireland, unemployment in, 12
North Sea products:
    effects on trade, 88
    oil output from, 13
    taxes on, 71-2
NUM, 51

OEEC, 92
oil prices, effect of 1973 rise in, 6
oil production, *see* North Sea
Oil Taxation Act, 1975, 71-2
output, comparative table of, 16
overdrafts, 76
overseas, decline in investment, 3
Overseas Sterling Area, 90

pension funds, 78
pensions, 52, 58-9
per capita income, 20
personal loans, 76, 77
PESC, 61
Petroleum Revenue Tax, 71-2
plastics industry, 31
Plowden Report (1961), 61
policy:
    allocation of materials, 110
    Common Agricultural (CAP), 6, 47, 49
    cycles, 115-16
        attempts to break, 116-20
    development of regional, 23-4
    education, 57-8
    employment, full, 107-8
    exchange rate, 93-4
    fiscal, definition of, 110-11

free trade, 3-6, 47
health and welfare, 55-7
housing, 59-60
incomes, 117-19
income distribution, 111
income support, 58-9
instruments, use of, in management of economy, 115-16
laissez-faire, 31-4
monetary, *see* monetary
New Towns, 26
N-I, 118
welfare and health, 55-7
population:
UK and US compared, 1
trends of UK, 1, 6-10
pottery, 33
power (energy), nationalization of, 72-4
Prais, S. J., 35
premium bonds, 79
price maintenance, resale, 39
Prices and Incomes Board, 74, 117
production:
data from census of, 36-7
of industrial sector, 29-34
productivity:
agreements, 117
changes in goods and services sector, 44
public authorities current expenditure, 15-16
public authority expenditure ratio, 64
public expenditure:
as a share of GDP, 16
on education, 57
on social services, 56
see also public finance
public finance, 61-74:
expenditure, changed patterns in, 61-6
nationalized industries, 72-4
taxation, 66-72:
capital (on personal income), 70-72
corporate, 68-9
selective employment, 69-70
value-added, 70
public sector, numbers of employees in, 15
purchase tax, 44

quarrying industry, changes in, 14-15, 29
quota system, decline of, 92

railways, nationalization of, 74
Reddaway, Professor W. B., 45
redundancy payments, 12
Regional Employment Premiums, 25, 69
regions:
comparative unemployment in, 12-13
variations in, 17-27
regulators, economic, 111
rent control, 60
Resale Prices Act (1964), 39
reserves, rapid rise in, 105
Restricted Trades Practices Act (1956), 39-41
royalties on oil, 72

sanitary arrangements (housing), 60
Save As You Earn scheme, 79
savings schemes, 79
school-leaving age, 57
Selective Employment Tax, 44, 69-70, 111
service industries:
growth of labour force in, 15
table of productivity in, 44
sector generally, 41-5
Sex Discrimination Act (1975), 55
shipbuilding industry, decline of, 4, 29
shipping receipts, 102
shop stewards, 51
sickness, 55-7, 58-9
Smith, A. D., (1972), 44
social issues, 50-60
policies, 55-60
education, 57-8
health and welfare, 55-7
housing, 59-60
income support, 58-9
trade unions and labour relations:
law, 53-5
liaison with government, 52-3
objectives, 51-2
structure and organization, 50-51
social security benefits, 56, 58-9
social services, public expenditure on, 56
South-East Region, steady growth of, 17-18
Special Development Areas, 25
see also Development Areas
state:
increase in intervention by, 4, 53, 111
legal framework for labour force, 53-5